# the
# hard
# good

# the hard good

showing up for God to work in
you when you want to shut down

## LISA WHITTLE

W PUBLISHING GROUP

AN IMPRINT OF THOMAS NELSON

Published in Nashville, Tennessee, by W Publishing Group, an imprint of Thomas Nelson.

The author is represented by Alive Literary Agency, www.aliveliterary.com.

Thomas Nelson titles may be purchased in bulk for educational, business, fund-raising, or sales promotional use. For information, please email SpecialMarkets@ThomasNelson.com.

Unless otherwise indicated, Scripture quotations are taken from the New International Version®, NIV®. © 1973, 1978, 1984, 2011 by Biblica, Inc.® Used by permission of Zondervan. All rights reserved worldwide.

Scripture quotations marked NLT are from the Holy Bible, New Living Translation. © 1996, 2004, 2015 by Tyndale House Foundation. Used by permission of Tyndale House Ministries, Carol Stream, Illinois 60188. All rights reserved.

Scripture quotations marked CSB are from the Christian Standard Bible. © 2017 by Holman Bible Publishers. Used by permission. Christian Standard Bible® and CSB® are federally registered trademarks of Holman Bible Publishers.

Scripture quotations marked ESV are from the ESV® Bible (The Holy Bible, English Standard Version®). © 2001 by Crossway, a publishing ministry of Good News Publishers. Used by permission. All rights reserved.

Scripture quotations marked KJV are from the King James Version. Public domain.

Scripture quotations marked NLV are from New Life Version. © 1969, 2003 by Barbour Publishing, Inc.

The use of italics in Scripture quotations are the author's own emphasis.

**Library of Congress Cataloging-in-Publication Data**

Names: Whittle, Lisa, author.
Title: The hard good : showing up for God to work in you when you want to shut down / Lisa Whittle.
Description: Nashville, Tennessee : W Publishing Group, an imprint of Thomas Nelson, 2021. | Includes bibliographical references. | Summary: "At our very core is the desire to be God's woman or man—faithful, having fulfilled the potential God created in us. To reach that point, sometimes we have to endure hard things, things God has designed for good, to supernaturally shape us into the people he wants us to be. When we choose to accept the "hard good," we discover our life's purpose, and he promises to give us the joy and passion as our deepest longing is fulfilled"— Provided by publisher.
Identifiers: LCCN 2021008828 (print) | LCCN 2021008829 (ebook) | ISBN 9780785232018 (paperback) | ISBN 9780785232025 (ebook)
Subjects: LCSH: Christian life. | Diligence. | Perseverance (Ethics) | Providence and government of God—Christianity.
Classification: LCC BV4509.5 .W465 2021 (print) | LCC BV4509.5 (ebook) | DDC 248.4—dc23
LC record available at https://lccn.loc.gov/2021008828
LC ebook record available at https://lccn.loc.gov/2021008829

*Printed in the United States of America*
21 22 23 24 25  LSC  10 9 8 7 6 5 4 3 2 1

*To my fathers in the two chairs of my heart . . .*
*Daddy: the irreplaceable original, who I miss every day*
*And John: the one I made room for*

# contents

# foreword

I WISH LIFE COULD JUST BE GOOD. FUN. PLEASANT. MEANINGFUL. Predictable but also adventurous. And that good would last forever—devoid of fear, anxiety, tragedy, heartbreak, betrayal, and grief.

But that's not the way life works. Maybe it's because we live in a sin-soaked world not capable of perfection. Or maybe it's because without the bitter, is it even possible to appreciate the sweet? Without the dark would the light ever be appreciated for the gift it is? And without the hard would we recognize the good as good?

I can't think of a person better equipped than my friend Lisa Whittle to tackle the hand-in-hand partnership of the title of this book: *The Hard Good*. She knows the angst of *hard* in deeply personal ways. She knows the choice of *good* because her heart purely seeks Jesus, and she truly wants to make a holy difference by helping others.

But it's in the combination of both words, *hard* and *good*, that she's learned to wear wisdom like that old sweatshirt that's your favorite because it's so broken in. At times life has broken Lisa, as it has all of us. But while fully acknowledging her heartbreak, she is equally committed to having it work for her and for a good that she pursues relentlessly.

I love her for that. And I am grateful to her since I need this reminder as much as anyone.

Once, while working out together (aka dying and trying to make sure your T-shirt stays pulled down to hide the obvious reality of the back side of life—insert big-eyed emoji), I was asking her questions about this book. I reversed the title and said to her, "Look at us doing the good hard things on this workout."

She graciously tilted her head and kindly corrected me, "hard good. End on the good. The hard is part of the journey, but the good is where we will land."

Brilliant.

I've thought of this conversation just about every day since.

Some things in my life right now are so hard I sometimes have to remind myself to exhale. I can find myself swept into a panic attack as unexpectedly as a person enjoying the beach one moment and swept away by a tsunami the next. And my deep desire for normalcy is sometimes hijacked by choices that aren't my own and yet affect me so deeply I want to hide in the nearest bathroom stall.

How can any of this be good?

I imagine you're asking this same question over something or someone in your life right now. And you're wondering if it is even worth it to try reading another book. After all, it's hard to get high on hope only to quickly get knocked down by your circumstances again, leaving your soul questioning everything. We need more than pat answers, plastic suggestions, and an author with too perfect of a life to truly understand our desperation. There is a lot at stake here.

Well, friend, breathe. Settle in. Dare to crack open these pages. Find a friend in Lisa that will be gentle when needed. Challenging when appropriate. And so very gracious as she cares for your pain. You can, as I do, trust her with your heart. Let's do this. Together we will discover the hard good is the best good—even if, especially if, you seriously doubt that right now. You'll soon see. This will be a book you keep on that one shelf signifying *never give this one away*. If you ever come over to my house, that's the shelf where mine will be.

Speaking of getting together, let's do that sometime! Me, you, and Lisa enjoying chips and queso and cupcakes. I mean, why not? You have a long T-shirt, right? Together we can do the hard good.

Love you!
—Lysa TerKeurst

# *why* i hope you read this book

---

I HAVE BEEN THINKING ABOUT THIS BOOK FOR ALMOST 1,825 DAYS, ever since my favorite person in the world got sick and died. That's when I started a journey of the *hard good*.

My hard-good story had in fact begun long before, but it wasn't until Dad developed a rare brain disorder and slipped away from us with a single breath that my keep-it-all-tucked-tightly-in-there heart was cracked open and God revealed to me how hard things didn't have to shut me down or make me bitter. Before that, I am not sure I could say hard things could also be good (or know how exactly that worked).

The reason this might matter to you is because your life is probably full of hard things, whether currently, in the future, or in the past . . . and you aren't over it.

But it's more than that. I definitely didn't know how hard things were the very keys to my growth process. That, as I had been praying for years, like "God, help me be more humble . . . less jealous . . . more open, loving, and kind . . . ," God would answer those prayers through the path of difficult circumstances. Perhaps you catch clues quicker than I do, but I didn't realize God was using this type of life as on-the-ground training-to-transformation. I find it's common to miss what is often right in front of us.

Our hard places are teaching us invaluable lessons while we are looking for a way to push them away.

If you want to know more about that, I hope you'll read this book.

If you want to get better and stop just existing . . . and even beyond that . . . if you want your life to matter beyond yourself, I hope you'll read this book.

I know right now you might feel as though everything is out of your control and life is simply handing you cards you cannot deal with. I agree that life does often deal us bad cards. This is the promise of God in John 16:33, that "in this world you will have trouble." We certainly know that.

But I hope you will come to know this too: though the world brings trouble, we do still have choice. Specifically, when it comes to our takeaway from the trouble life brings.

God wants to make much of your life. He has anointed and appointed you for a special purpose, yes, even knowing about the hard that would come your way. But you will determine your level of usability for the kingdom of God in how you respond to it.

God also has a great purpose for your life, and that has never changed. It is my belief, based on Scripture, His purpose is the same for every believer (read the book to find out what that is if you don't know!), which might come as a surprise to you. The reason a lot of us make only slim progress in our lives is because we are searching for something that is set (purpose), rather than pursuing our *usability*, which is up to each of us—and what I have firmly come to believe is developed in the things we discuss in *The Hard Good*.

And that is where you find this book: helping us see our hard circumstances—less hard to unbearably hard on the scale but all humanly difficult—for the good that can result from them. But only with God. That is the deal breaker.

So here are the two last things I want you to know.

1. If you truly want what you say you want in life (Joy! Peace! Love! Hope! Fulfillment! Purpose!), you will have to stay with God through the uncomfortable process to get there. There's no way around. Up to now, you may have thought that the reason you never got anywhere was because life is too hard. But the real reason is because when life gets hard, you keep bailing on where God wants to take you, and you keep having to start over. I hope, instead, you choose not to start over and let the process in this book move you forward. Progress is priceless. It also carries with it the gift of peace. I talk a lot about my father in this book, an endless thrasher who truly found peace in the latter years of his life when he no longer could physically run away; his spirit followed suit, and he was a better man for it. The lessons I learned from watching this process come out now in these pages.

2. If you truly want to be spiritually transformed, you have to redefine *good*. Right now, you may well be operating under a faulty definition of *good*. Culture has a loud voice, and it's hard to hear truth over it. What we've heard are all the mantras: *You are good, just as you are. You create your own good life.* I'd love for those things to be true, but they simply aren't. Just because God loves and accepts us as we are, and just because He has given us many gifts and capabilities, doesn't mean we can swing the pendulum to a destructive narrative of self-heroism. The lies about the good life are pretty but covertly exhausting. It also has us thinking we have done something wrong if we don't have a "good life" like someone else. Creating a good life takes a lot of hard

work and isn't sustainable long-term. Thankfully the Bible provides the common sense we need and gives us a different definition of good—centered not on us or our strength or capabilities but on *God*.

- God is good. Therefore, hard things that lead you to God will be good for you.
- Growth is good. That means that you can't be good without process and progress.
- A good life = a life of kingdom usability. Not fame, fortune, or ease.

And what may be the most important thing to note from that quotable in Romans 8: "All things work together for good" (v. 28 KJV): the most missed word in the verse is *together*, and it's the most important. It does not say that all things *work out*. It says all things work *together*. This means that there will be missteps, disappointments, losses, and things that fall through along the way. Not everything in this world will work out for us. But the hard things will work together for good for those who love God and desire to be usable for His kingdom.

So then what is our role with good if it's all about God? It comes back to that uncomfortable process. It is to stay with God on that journey (hard) He has ordained to transform us (good), not to create a journey for ourselves (we can't, anyway). It is a dependent versus a director role. (PS: Expect the world to disagree.)

So, yes, good is the crucial end here. It is the God-defined one found in godly growth, not in self-gratification or glory. The irony is that godly growth will bring the gratification we have been looking for our whole lives.

And it is, indeed, *a sweet life*. Because unlike a limited good life we might try to make for ourselves by avoiding godly growth through the refinement process, the hard-good process is an alternative for pointless pain and exhaustion. If hard is going to be a part of my life, and it's proven that it is, I prefer for it to have produced something. I suspect you agree.

*I'm praying* The Hard Good *will help heal you.* We are a tired bunch, and I don't just mean needing sleep. I see you, worn down by life. I see you, brokenhearted. I see you, trying your best. I see you, sick of this same issue . . . over yourself. I see you, wanting to get close to God. I see you, notorious bailer. I see you, scared and lonely. I see you, reaching out for help. Here's the beauty of the hard good: If you feel life has been unfair to you, you can be right. But at the same time, you don't have to concede that life has won. We are doing something new, today, even with unwashed hair.

*I'm praying* The Hard Good *will help change you.* Right now, your first goal may not be for God to use you. You may simply be trying to recover from something, or clinging to the hope that better days are ahead. But at some point, you'll need more than just hanging on. You'll want what's left of your life to matter. When you get to that place, this book will be helpful for you too.

*God, help our hearts who seek your transformative way.*
*Here we are.*
*Here we go.*

CHAPTER 1

## accepting something you wish were something different

All pain's a prelude: to symphony, to sweetness.
"The pearl began as a pain in the
oyster's stomach."
—EUGENE H. PETERSON[1]

*January 2019*

I'M SITTING IN A RESTAURANT WHERE IT WOULD BE A SIN NOT TO order the fish, a place overlooking the bay with walls painted in all manner of ocean life. As is becoming my new norm, this evening is a most joyously awkward occasion. Two years ago my favorite person in the world, my father, died. And now I'm here with my mother and her newlywed husband, John.

To make the night's dinner even more sweetly complicated, we've been joined by some of my favorite people—most of my dad's brothers and sisters, who happen to live close by. Everyone's here to eat and catch up, and all but me are of the sixty-five-and-over crowd. John is in his happy place, and just knowing him the short time I have, I would bet my last one hundred dollars he will order the shrimp. (I would have won the bet.) This place is one of John's favorites, and he and Mom are regulars.

I call John my bonus dad after some back-and-forth discussion with my mother and despite her hope I would call him Brother John like most of his longtime church congregants. I resisted that idea, and she subsequently conceded. John is a pastor—was a pastor, for fifty-four years—and when you pastor for that long, I am of the opinion it's not fair to lose that title. But the whole dad-titling thing has been a hard, strange, different story.

We laugh, talk, and eat far too many hush puppies, along with those Club crackers that come before the meal in any fish place worth its salt. John tells preacher stories I've already heard to infinity. I stare at my aunt's profile, which looks hauntingly like my own. Drifting into another world, I glance out the big glass window at a seabird power-walking frantically for a crumb, and I suddenly wish to join him. Everyone on the other end of the table is happy and laughing, but my heart feels detached from the current joy. *It's too loud in here. The jokes and stories are dumb. Please, no one notice I'm not participating, and especially, please don't say my name and make me join in.*

I'm happy they are happy, but I am not happy that everyone's hearts seem to be faring better than my own. My decision to choose the farthest seat by the window is proving the best place to escape with my thoughts into the outdoors and is even more brilliant because it puts me next to Uncle Wade, the greatest uncle of all time. Though just his brother-in-law, Uncle Wade reminds me more than anyone of Dad. His big hands, assertive nature, and memories almost always involving Sansabelt pants. It's been forty years, but if I close my eyes, I can see the black-headed duo, Dad and Wade, aggressively herding us kids along during holiday family reunions. Dad's yelling, *"Mach schnell!"* German words he picked up from his father and probably the only ones he could repeat in front of us kids. He had a few years on Wade, and Wade idolized him. Everyone idolized Daddy.

Or maybe that was just me.

And now here we all are, Uncle Wade, most of the Reimer siblings, Bonus Dad, and Mom. Even that bird outside has shown up for a party.

But the one person I want is conspicuously gone.

No matter how old we are or how much time we had with them, losing someone we love leaves us with a deep sense of longing.

Suddenly and without warning, my head becomes heavy for a place to lie, and it finds Uncle Wade's shoulder. I'm forty-six years old, but I am not. I'm six years old again, and Uncle Wade is my daddy. I know he's not. He doesn't feel the same. But he is, right now, because I need him to be. Tears trickle, and I can do nothing to stop them. This is the wrong moment to cry; John is midway through a good story. Too bad tears never listen. I let my head lie for as long as it needs. Long enough to find rest.

> *No matter how old we are or how much time we had with them, losing someone we love leaves us with a deep sense of longing.*

Finally my head rises, even while the tears still stream. A smile cracks, without permission. The irony of the moment has not escaped me. *Daddy would love this.*

My daddy, Jim Reimer, moved our family all over the blessed United States, so much so that only a map and the four hearts who rode in the U-Hauls could live to tell it. It was always his dream to move us near his family, this Texas bunch he loved so deeply. But we never made it to live near them except one year when I was in the fifth grade, which was the year I got mono, so I barely remember a thing except not seeing them much after all. And now, this is where Mom lives—in the very same Texas city but without him. With her new husband instead, who also happened to be Dad's good friend. (Keep reading, I'll tell you all about that.)

Over the course of time since Mom started dating John, I've now seen Dad's family more than I probably ever saw them growing up. And tonight we're together, eating shrimp. If there was ever a time I hoped someone could see down from heaven, it's this very moment. No one would love this more than my dad—seeing everyone he loved so much in one place.

Absence and presence. Loss and gain. Deep pain and deep love. Living in the tension of *the hard good*.

Since I was little, it was my daddy who told me I could do anything, and he assured me Jesus would help me do it. He was right. I'm doing something very hard: laughing and loving and accepting a life without him. I wish he could see me now.

You know how you feel when you finally stop pushing back in your heart against something you have been resisting that has been exhausting you?

That's how I felt when I stopped pushing back on the idea of fully accepting my life without Dad and one that included John. This night was a moment in that journey.

Turns out I can miss my daddy and love the bonus dad I have at the same time.

It is hard to accept something we wish were different. But when we do, we exchange pain for freedom.

## When You Wish It Were Something Different

April 2, 2017, was the last time I saw my father alive. Ever since that crisp Sunday morning when he left us to go live the better life in heaven, the clock started on a new life of acceptance for all of us who loved him. The four-year acceptance clock has been a real teacher. One of the things I've learned: death is an intruder who rudely interrupts plans, wishes, and dreams, and it certainly cares nothing about relationships you've worked hard on. I knew fifty-two years of marriage was bonding for my parents, but until I saw my mother whisper and weep over my father's body with him already gone, I never really knew. That day I saw till death do us part—a love far deeper than it is on a wedding day.

I've also come to realize that acceptance of something we wish were something different is, perhaps, hardest for humans because of our hidden belief that somehow, if we reject things, even in our mind, we prevent them from being true. *Control*, if you prefer the one-word answer. Except for the one nagging problem: life isn't up for bargaining. My theory is that if we knew what acceptance actually was (and the good it does, which I'll get to later), we might be more open to it. It is our choice for better mental and emotional health, not the ability to play God in the decision-making. It also does not mean that just because I understand it, I still don't miss my dad.

*October 29, 2018*

*Daddy showed up in my dreams last night.*

He was so real he could've popped out of my favorite photo of him sitting on my desk. Dark '70s pinstripe suit, thick black hair combed neatly to one side, tanned cheeks, and perfect, full lips.

Impossibly good-looking, as always. Except in my dream he wasn't touching a chair and looking so stately. He was reaching out to hold me and looking warmly into my eyes.

This was the first time I've seen him in more than a year and a half. Every day since he took that last breath, I've wished he were still alive.

I don't want you to think you're alone in having a hard time accepting something (or someone). In case you thought my story at the fish restaurant was precious, and before you assume my acceptance of John becoming my bonus dad was all kisses and hugs, you should know this: nobody has a love story like me and my daddy.

Every daddy's girl probably thinks that, at least when we are six and he is the greatest man we know. Daddy and I had the unspoken thing in the eyes from day one, and we kept it until he was so sick it became the one and only way he could speak to me. We communicated a lot in body language through the years. A nod, a knowing grin. We spoke in the language of commonality and the heart although it looked different in the end when his liberty to talk was stripped away. (A preacher losing his voice, of all cruel ironies.) We were Court TV junkies, always up on the latest news, neither of us lacking fire or opinion. Both of us for the underdog, fiercely loyal to our people yet tender to the bone. I've never loved a soul like my daddy, my whole life.

I loved another man since, my husband, who wound up loving my dad almost as much as I did (which became one of my greatest gifts), but never anyone identically. I got Dad, and he got me. I knew he was good even though he sometimes fought wanting to be bad. I knew he held secrets, probably stuff from his past that would hurt me too much to know. I knew he loved us to the very best of his ability, more than he had been equipped to do himself because of his relationship with his dad. And I knew something else: he loved me special, whatever that meant. He told me this many times even though he deeply loved all his kids.

I believe God had me know him like this so I could write his story.

Daddy was average height, but he was thick. Manly, aggressive, alpha in every way. He *was* the big gun he shot deer with, loud and powerful. He *was* the big truck he drove, sleek and commanding. He *was* the big pulpit he preached behind, charismatic and strong. There was no middle ground with Daddy. He was the renegade, the advocate, and the one every person either was dying to get near or strongly disliked. I've met speakers far more famous than he was but none more electric.

I learned early on what Christian celebrity looked like, long before the social media influencer age, because a Christian celebrity lived in my home.

Daddy was simultaneously buddies with the church janitor and lunch mates with the town mayor. Endearing and polarizing. Absent and dependable. An open book and fiercely private. A true living irony. My father's very life preached to me that two seemingly opposite things could indeed live together at the same time, just like hard and good.

He was complicated and, at times, unstable. So our life with him was full and rich yet complicated and, at times, unstable too.

When I was eighteen, the pedestal my daddy occupied in my mind broke into a million pieces, and he fell hard onto the ground where the rest of us lived. A friend of mine revealed to me one cold Missouri night that she was sure he was having an affair with someone I knew, and she had receipts to prove it. For reasons I still cannot fully explain, though I had loved my father my whole life, something told me to believe her, so I did. The news broke me—I did not think I would recover from the pain in my heart. My daddy, the one I thought I knew, the one I loved the very most, had deceived us all. What a fool I was.

Here's something I found out: when we react out of pain against someone who hurts us by turning inward, we turn the knife against ourselves. I didn't tell my daddy he hurt me in words. Instead, I screamed at him silently by doing things to hurt him back— dating bad boys, blowing my grades, lying to his face about where I was going, getting drunk at parties. All the things good preachers' daughters shouldn't do. Every day for about a year, I shoved my anguish in his face without saying a word, hoping he would notice. But by now I was also a good liar, so between that and being busy, Daddy never noticed. This broke me some more.

And then one day, after my sins caught up with me and I could no longer carry on hurting myself, I made a decision that changed my life. I decided to stop wondering if my father had an affair. I realized that I might never know the truth, and either way it didn't matter. Because this didn't have to mess up our love story. I loved him for who he was to me. I loved him for the memories in his huge black truck, the trips to Subway, the way we knew what each other was thinking with a nod and a grin. These things remained true. If the affair was also true, the forgiveness was ultimately God's and my mother's to give. Not mine. I would probably never know the full story, so I let the story go. I accepted the not knowing.

I accepted this father, the flawed version I now knew. I even accepted what I came to call "the night," the time I heard about his alleged affair—a memory I'd often wished away whenever it replayed in my mind.

This was the first time I remember accepting something I wished were something different and feeling set free.

Maybe this is not your exact story, but you can relate to feeling that you must let go of the need to know about something. This is an important place of acceptance. It is a transformational moment in and of itself because, in a strange twist, as we let something go, we unloose something that has gripped us. It is also a place we often get stuck—we want to, but we fight it all the way because it feels as if something holding the cards over our life has won. We will not accept not knowing why, why not, or the details. But it truly is one of the most powerful practices when we let go of that need to know. It isn't conceding to do so. It is taking power back from the endless question mark that has punctuated every sentence of our lives.

## PROBLEM #1: You Can't Accept Life Because You Can't Accept You

We don't need a perfect bow tied around our stories to be okay.

Even if something doesn't become different, you can live with it. Love your life, even, *despite*.

This is another place we get stuck: we reject our lives because they are not perfect. We don't really believe, deep down, that we can be okay with a less than perfect job, marriage, house, kids, or church, so we stay on a constant hunt or in constant dissatisfaction. Our bent to fix things (aka control or take matters into our own hands) convinces us that to be okay with something, it must first be altered to our level of preference.

It is why our family was basically the Reimer Traveling Band when I was growing up—"gypsies," my mom used to jokingly call us from time to time, except there was no fun band. We just moved. To the tune of double digits, by the time I was in sixth grade, which eventually started to feel normal. My father was trying to "fix" a life that wasn't broken but he wasn't willing to fully accept. Turns out when you try to fix a life with a moving van, you just pack up and move the issues to a different address.

You willing to dive in with me a bit further? The real thing that was happening with my father was *he couldn't truly accept himself, so accepting his life was then out of the question.* At the core, acceptance of anything can almost always be traced back to some level of acceptance of ourselves. It is usually not about the first thing we blame it on.

Maybe the biggest problem hasn't been your life being a bad life, after all. Maybe it hasn't been that you're not suited for this career, you've had rotten luck, or you don't have the opportunity to turn things around. Maybe you *are* equally gifted to that person you admire and God *does* love you as much as someone else. Maybe you just haven't accepted *you* or God loving you, and that has blocked all other acceptance.

I sensed early on that Daddy didn't believe he was fully loved by God. At least, not in the way that allows a person to accept who they are. This is tied into your entire self-acceptance. Dad's wild boyhood, rebellious youth, and unbridled Navy days were stuck in his head, constantly replaying his unworthiness. This caused a lot of complications—performance issues, running away, and hiding his truth, to name a few—and stifled his full potential. He accomplished a lot while he was here—preached thousands of sermons and influenced an equal number of lives. Many of his sermons were full of powerful words about how much God loves us. He certainly repeated the same message at home to me. Yet I watched him silently wrestle. He lived with unspoken guilt and shame demons—the pesky ones that try to get you to hate yourself by mental reminders that wear you down. I well know the life of a front-row spectator to a man's spiritual battle.

It's important for me, then, to make sure *you* now know that everything you struggle to accept in your life will be easier when you believe God loves you. This is foundational. It is nearly impossible to accept a life if you do not first accept being purposefully born into it and if you believe you can't live in the tension of being loved versus feeling loved. Sometimes our humanness throws up baggage barricades that block our receiving end.

I suspect a lot of us are like my father—worn down by mental reminders that hinder our ability to fully experience God's love, so we treat ourselves poorly. This is crucial to note because acceptance and guilt can't coexist. A lot of us want to accept something different about our story, but we are our own worst personal historian. Sometimes we need to take our own history book out back and make a nice campfire out of its pages. Once you've learned where you came from, and how it affected you, those roads don't need to constantly be retraveled. This is different from owning past sin and mistakes and seeking repentance—a necessary piece of moving on. But many of us still struggle even after we've given something over to God, which was the case with my dad.

If you relate to this, may I suggest you start with this two-word question: *What now?*

When *what was* becomes *what now*, it becomes a power move in the right direction.

Take a page from my father's book: if you find yourself chronically dissatisfied with your life, make sure it's not you who you're actually running from, spending year after year chasing after new adventures. The need to accept yourself could also stem from something else. Rather than running from past mistakes or guilt, maybe you wish you were somehow created differently. I relate to that.

I didn't want to be me for years. I wanted to be my mother. I wanted a personality other people had a hard time rejecting, misunderstanding, or getting mad at, which she has. Instead, my little-girl frame had a fire stuck inside with nowhere to go, so I ended up inserting myself inconveniently into conversations in which feistiness was not welcome. We may still have further to go in the church when it comes to women, but growing up in the '80s with passionate gifting wasn't the plight a young girl wanted, I'll tell you that.

This whole book could be about my struggle to accept my body, something women are notoriously lifelong strugglers over, no matter how hard we try (prayer does help!). Speaking from experience, people born with the gift of a healthy body can become grossly entitled, nitpicking ourselves to death by the view from our blessed lens. When you don't have to worry about legs that work, you have the luxury of hating the way they look too thick at the ankle. (Teary and sorrowful as I write this.) This leads to such self-loathing and ingratitude. I hated my short legs my whole life. Cruelly pushed them to get them thinner. I've been on every diet that exists, not to mention bulimia and excessive exercise. I've never typed those words before now. But after what I put myself through in college, I owe my body at least enough to say it. Over the years I've come to accept the legs I have, something no amount of deprivation or dieting will change. Yes, you *can* live with things you didn't ask for. Gratitude doesn't require preference; it requires acceptance.

You don't have to choose between knowing your life isn't perfect and being grateful for it anyway. Those two things are equally true. Accepting the parts you don't love will help shape you into a person who no longer needs everything to be perfect.

Maybe you've been waiting your whole life for that magical moment when you finally feel differently about something like a body part. But what if you never do? Or maybe it's something you've done that you keep wishing to redo instead of learning to accept. We can fix a lot of things in this modern age, but we can't fix a broken past we are trying to outrun. The good news for those of us who haven't had a great start is this: we choose our level of wellness even when we don't choose every detail of our life. Yes, even when something broke us. Yes, even when someone behaves poorly in our presence. Still. Yes, even when we are reminded of the something every single day because it is part of us.

Accepting things about ourselves we wish were different is the key to accepting the totality of our life. Nothing is well if we aren't at peace with ourselves.

If you're in need of greater belief about or acceptance of something related to you, the ability to do both is covered by the truth of Ephesians 1—in that radical move of Jesus to give us, as children of God, access to the same power that has the *power to resurrect*.

> I pray that the eyes of your heart may be enlightened in order that you may know the hope to which he has called you, the riches of his glorious inheritance in his holy people, and his incomparably great power for us who believe. That power is the same as the mighty strength he exerted when he raised Christ from the dead and seated him at his right hand in the heavenly realms, far above all rule and authority, power and dominion, and every name that is invoked, not only in the present age but also in the one to come. (vv. 18–21)

Game-changing news. Satan may have a lot of us believing we are doomed to weakness, but I'm outing the lie. In many cases we aren't waiting on circumstances. We're waiting on our minds and hearts to change. That's where the power starts. Can you believe we've been waiting on something we didn't need to wait on?

Demanding of ourselves that we be sold on everything about us before we accept it is a big ask. Life is too good to be put on hold by our expectations for perfect circumstances. This is not settling. It's letting go of a standard that's been toxic to our soul. It's not simply waving a white flag but a willful laying down of a life that's too long been driven by things outside our control. Acceptance means harnessing the power we already own (Ephesians 1!) and choosing to move on despite preference. It's choosing health and sanity and a more joyful life. I like this news because it means that nothing outside of God owns my future, and yet with Him, things can happen right here and now.

If you've been living under the belief that acceptance requires prior alterations or being completely sold on everything about yourself first, here's your permission to now think differently.

## PROBLEM #2: You Can't Accept Two Things Being True at the Same Time

Living with the demand that only one thing can be true at a time will hinder you. It is crucial to your entire ability to believe good things can also be hard. If both can't be true (*this is/was hard, but God can also use it for my good . . . this was something I never wanted, but God can redeem it*), we are left with many hollow days and eventual ineffectiveness. While we may never *understand* the process, we can still *believe in* the process as we believe in God. Another example of holding two truths at one time.

Please hear me. This is not the same as Satan's marketing of two very different things—one true and one false/anti-gospel—via culture, wrapping them together so that truth morphs into humanism. *We should not live to please other people* (absolutely true and biblical); *therefore, we should do exactly what we want to do* (anti-gospel). We will talk more about this prevalent theme in today's society later in the chapter. We must wisely divide these things to get to the truth. The key phrase is holding *two truths* at the same time, not *one truth and one lie.*

My social media tells the tale of two truths that live together in a singular moment: in fact, hard, as I read about one friend's enormous grief at the anniversary of her child's death, and good, while moments later I watch a video of another friend shooting off a makeshift backyard cannon full of pink dye, announcing her pregnancy. Life is about that coexistence.

If you want to have a usable, powerful life, you have to begin to accept its nuances.

Sometimes life will have you laughing five minutes after you've cried.

Sometimes you will be close to God, and at the same time, you will still struggle with human feelings.

Sometimes you will be mad at your circumstances and feel grateful to still be alive.

And this goes for others too. Give them the grace you give yourself to be living the reality of more than just one thing.

We all are.


## PROBLEM #3: You Can't Accept Someone or Something in Your Life

I didn't pick John to come into our family. In fact, when Dad died, we weren't looking *at all* for another family member to join us.

Some months after my father's passing, Mom mentioned John to me for the first time. We were sitting in the parking lot of the attorney's office having just sorted out some things in her will when she casually slid it into our conversation. "Remember John Morgan?"

Only minutes before, we had been discussing things like powers of attorney around a mahogany table. Dad's death had brought on hard, necessary conversations about her future, postponed by his more immediate health concerns. Now that he was gone, we could deal with things. After sorting through details and before going our separate ways for the night, we were spending a few minutes catching up. Mom and I lived just around the corner from each other, and we talked nearly every day, at least through text. But for a week or so I'd been sensing she had been trying to tell me something.

"Of course," I said.

John was a friend of Dad's—a close friend, although they hadn't seen each other in years. In the ministry world, you could have friends like that. He was a preacher friend, running in the same denominational circles, someone Dad considered a great pastor and perhaps the smartest financial leader around. Long before today's popular financial gurus, John was helping folks get out of debt in his down-to-earth, unflashy way, and teaching his own church to stay debt-free. He was also a hunting friend, with a mutual affection for the majesty of deer antlers. A true cowboy who, like Dad, wore real cowboy boots and hats, drove big trucks, and hunted everything from rattlesnakes to grizzly bear. I'd met John several times as a teenager, including during that short stint when we lived in Houston and I was sick for months with that crazy mono. We had attended John's church, although I don't remember it.

Through the years I had also heard a story involving John, one that deeply touched my heart. Back in the late '80s, my father got in trouble with the state's hunting and game commission, having broken a federal law by transporting a deer head over state lines. (If only Dad had known that apparently he could have bought a permit for less than ten dollars.) He sold it to John for his collection, so when the deer head was confiscated in a raid after the IRS stepped in, John was out both the deer head and a large sum of money. (Like fine art, deer heads are worth a lot.) Nearly bankrupt from legal fees, back taxes, penalties, and interest owed to the federal government, Dad didn't have any way to pay John back. But John forgave the debt without a further word. Even more incredibly, he continued being Dad's friend. Ironically, the last time Dad preached at a sportsmen's event was at John's church. After that, his health declined to the point he could no longer speak publicly again. Knowing what I know now, the divine timing of this last speaking engagement doesn't escape me.

"What about John Morgan?" I asked my mother.

Hands twisting in her lap, she looked at me tentatively. "John's wife died a month after Dad. He's been calling me. We've been talking . . . a lot . . . these last few weeks."

I didn't need to ask her about what. I could tell by her face. Suddenly a lot of things made sense. They both lost spouses of fifty-plus years just a month apart. They both dearly loved my dad. With the vast knowledge only he had, after Dad died, both John and his wife had reconnected with Mom upon the request of Dad's brother (a mutual friend of John's) to help Mom get rid of Dad's remaining deer heads. Dad and John shared similar faith and belief systems. Being in the same denomination and era, they even had mutual ministry friends. It all added up. They were deeply compatible. And it felt right, somehow ordained by a Power much greater than any of us, even to a mind that didn't want to accept that any of it was true or necessary. I was still freshly wrapping my mind around my father being gone. And I was enjoying having my mother, who had for years given herself fully to his caretaking, back in a daily, active relationship.

I didn't say it at the time, but that day in the parking lot I knew what would one day come. A year and a half later, Mom and John were married in a private ceremony.

I know what it's like to want someone but learn to accept someone different.

I know what it feels like to have to embrace someone new even as you still wish for the one who is gone.

Sometimes the thing we wish were something different is a person, and the weight of that can feel particularly hard. It can feel like betrayal of the person we wish for, loved first, knew the longest, committed to back when. And now, even though it's not within our power to have them in our lives, acceptance of someone new feels nearly impossible. It is not wrong to struggle to accept. It is human. This is why we need a supernatural God to help bridge the gaps in our hearts.

The beauty of acceptance is we find out how well a closed heart can open and a broken heart can mend. We grow when we defy the beliefs that have made us live below our potential to do such things. And then we crave growth some more. It is a cycle of transformation and healing, a place where God is able to begin to greatly use us.

> *The beauty of acceptance is we find out how well a closed heart can open and a broken heart can mend.*

Maybe for you it's a stepparent you've yet to accept. A new pastor, because you pine for the old one. Adjusting to a new spouse or a new normal in a long marital relationship you are asking God to mend after an affair.

Maybe you struggle to accept someone because they aren't that lovable, or they've hurt you in some way. Even if that someone isn't worthy of your love and acceptance right now, you can let go of your need for the demand of that. Being a worthiness judge is simply too draining of a job. And if they have not been healthy for your life, well, I assume you know about the importance of boundaries.

And for the one who *is* worthy of your love but you just don't want to see it right now so you are resisting: Please don't miss out on the someone right in front of you because you are too busy wishing for someone else. Or simply because you feel the need to push back on the idea of new memories. You may never have asked for this gift, but will you trust God to know what you need?

He knows what we need with circumstances, too, like a job we don't get, a relationship that falls through that we were sure was going to wind up in marriage, even some injustice we can't make right. A lot of us have wandered for years, racking our brains for a way to home-remedy our pain over these huge disappointments. It won't work. I've tried the quick fixes myself, so I can say that.

For us, the need for acceptance is often about letting go of an offense, even toward our own life. Yes, you heard me right. *Our circumstances have offended us.* (Hear me out if at first this sounds strange.) A lot of us are in a cycle of offense over something that has happened to us, and, because of that, we refuse to accept anything that comes after. Essentially we are stuck at the point of the something we wish were different in our circumstances, and we have not progressed forward. Four words have become our life mantra: *I can't believe it.* This is the thought that is in the back of our minds every day as we try to progress forward, dream, live, serve God, and love other people. No wonder we find it difficult to produce and always have so much on our minds. Underlying thoughts of disappointment keep us in mental cycles of being mad at our lives. Acceptance is the way to break that.

I'd like to offer one more thing that might help us as it relates to other people in this regard. The ramifications for a lack of acceptance affect more than just us. Because we have a hard time accepting our own circumstances, we tend sometimes to say really dumb things to other people in their pain over things that are hard to accept. God seems to be the most logical go-to for the why of circumstances, so we tend to carelessly throw His name around. One time, when my friend was pregnant with her son, someone tried to tell her that God had meant for her husband to cheat on her while pregnant to get her attention. Knowing what I know about God, I feel sure He could have chosen other methods to get in touch besides one that resulted in an STD, my friend going into premature labor, and a marriage breaking up. God isn't responsible for man's choice though, as our Creator, He anticipates the fallenness and stands ready with the help. We will cover so much more about hard circumstances in the coming chapters of this book, but the one thing you can count on is that as you accept what you didn't ask for or want, it changes you for the good—it does not affirm an unwelcome decision.

*As you accept what you didn't ask for or want, it changes you for the good.*

In that way, disappointment and pain become a very strange but powerful gift.

Nearly a year after my father's death, when Mom had quietly started dating John, I flew to Texas with my family and mother so we could get truly acquainted and he could meet my husband and kids. After months of private grappling, late-night prayers, and tears for God to help me accept this new man in my mother's life, and even as I mourned for the man I wanted but couldn't make come back, something surprising happened to me that weekend. John's schedule kept him going at a rigorous pace, even in his late seventies, and he rarely got sick, but John wasn't feeling well on our visit. Hearing him cough, looking into tired eyes, and knowing he was sick, I found myself worrying about him, a man I barely knew.

Feelings of love washed over me. As I sat on his back deck watching him talk and laugh with my family like an old friend, my mind brought me a thought. "There's room." I knew what that meant, and it meant a lot. He wasn't my father, and he never would be. I hadn't stopped wishing my father were still here. But I had space in my heart for John Morgan too. I *could* accept the man standing right in front of me. And God could use it to change me.

Sometimes we have more room in our heart than we think.

Have you made room for yourself?

Have you made room for someone you never went looking for or circumstances you didn't prefer?

Most important: Will you choose to believe that though acceptance is hard, it is a powerful good that God can use in your life to shape you?

I hope you at least said yes to the last one because I'm about to show you more.

## ཏ GOOD: ༄
**Your defeating *what ifs* will turn into joy over *what is*.**

---

*If you are tired and ready to lose some inner turmoil, be willing to eliminate these two words from your life: what if.*

---

Our defeating *what ifs* are most often centered on these three questions:

*What if they . . .?*
*What if I . . .?*
*What if God . . .?*

See if any of these common questions sound familiar: What if I had more money? What if I had been born into a different family or with a different personality? What if I hadn't wasted those years? What if God had stopped that tragedy from happening? What if God had given me what He gave them? What if they hadn't hurt me? What if they had given me another chance? The list goes on.

*What ifs* hinder us as we journey through life. They stifle our motivation, hold us back from progress, and keep God's greatest work from being done in and through our lives.

As you do the hard work of accepting things you wish were different, know it is not for naught: it is to your great benefit. Your defeating *what ifs* will turn into joy over *what is* as you release expectations of controlling something uncontrollable. It is a most worthy exchange of power.

In this exchange your hard transforms into something good. As support to this hard-good process, I find it particularly helpful to pray the serenity prayer by American theologian Reinhold Niebuhr. Perhaps you know it.

> *God, grant me the serenity to accept the things I*
> *cannot change,*
> *courage to change the things I can,*
> *and wisdom to know the difference.*

I remember hearing this prayer in college, back when I was in the throes of being manically self-critical. A bad relationship with an equally critical boyfriend sent me into mental loops about my body, which led me to food deprivation. I tried to receive the truth of the prayer. But I felt helpless, as if maybe I could never accept the things I was stuck with, and that sent me further into rejection of myself.

When we are in a state of denying acceptance to ourselves about one thing, the list of critiques can grow incredibly silly.

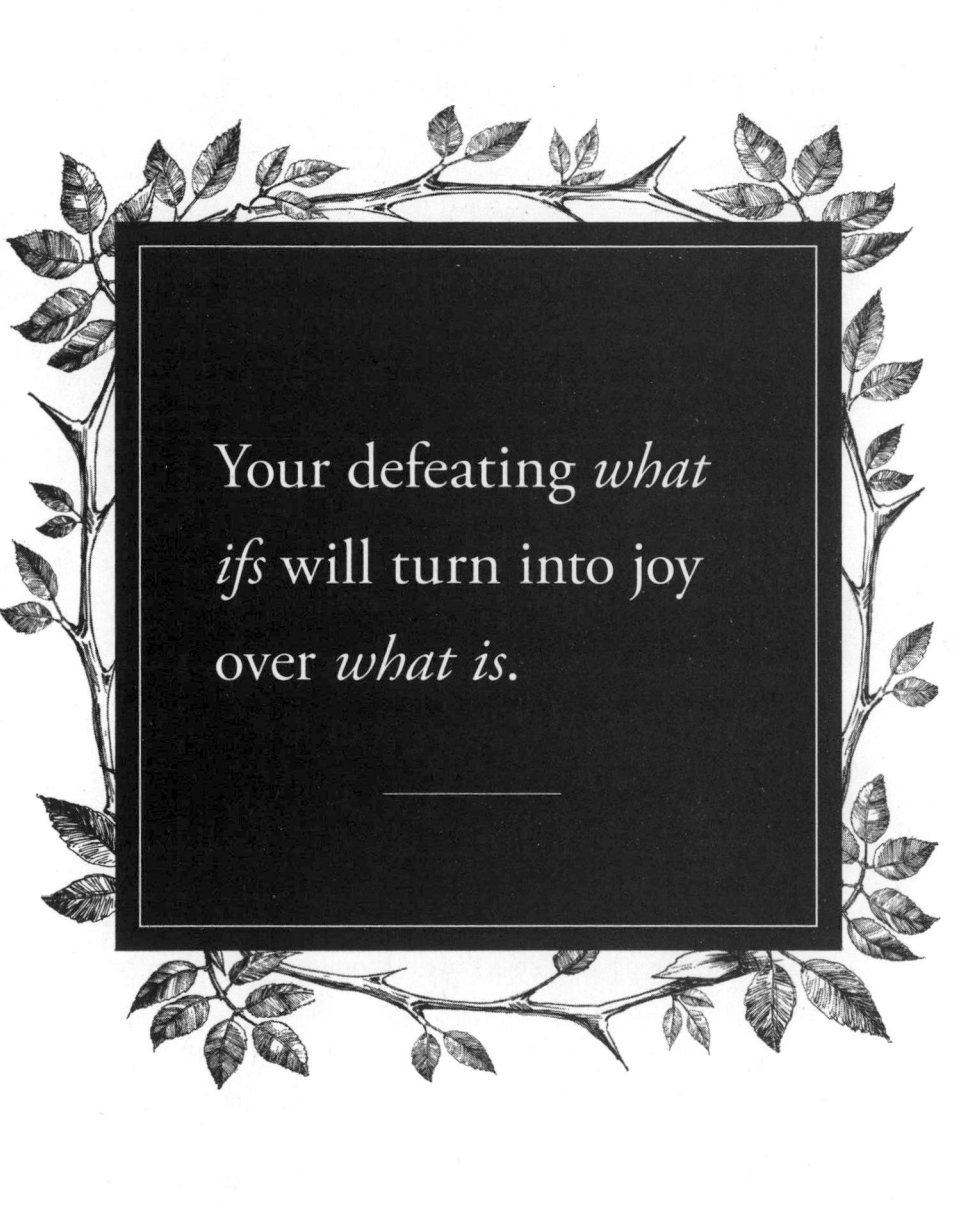

Your defeating *what ifs* will turn into joy over *what is*.

Our cruelty to ourselves snowballs. Fast. Before we know it, we're rejecting things about ourselves that normally would have never made the list. That's the irony about human acceptance: the more we look to a source other than God for peace, the less peaceful we will be.

*The serenity to accept the things I cannot change.*

Serenity is defined simply in some places as "the state of being untroubled." This helps me understand what my goal is in accepting something I don't prefer. To be untroubled about something doesn't mean I necessarily like it any more than I did at first. It means I do not let it overwhelm my thoughts and take over my life. No disrespect to Niebuhr, but this isn't a new idea. It's the very words of Jesus to His disciples when He was preparing to leave the earth. "Do not let your hearts be troubled," He said, over an intimate dinner meant to comfort them before He went away (John 14:1).

They couldn't change His going. They couldn't stop fear of the great unknown from creeping in. But they had the power within them, through trust in Jesus, to live with untroubled hearts in acceptance of *what was*. Despite their natural desire to have the Lord physically present with them. No doubt they lived with the rub of these two truths long after He was gone.

Don't let the parallels to our own current reality escape you. We're living in the same difficult world with the same Lord inside us, longing to have His tangible, physical comfort. Sometimes not having a God we can touch leaves us frustrated, wishing for more. I get that, and, more importantly, He does too. But this is where faith grows. We can experience the closeness of His presence even while wishing for more. And we will get it one day, in heaven, which keeps us from getting too comfortable down here.

We, too, can choose to live untroubled, despite the troubles we cannot change. Living untroubled while surrounded by trouble is possible only with a God perspective. And, yes, it *is* possible.

### *Courage to change the things I can.*

As a there-is-always-a-way-it-can-be-done type of person, I love this part of the serenity prayer. Victimization doesn't sit well with me. If it's in my power to change something, ten times out of ten, I will. You may not share my personality, but you probably share the universal need not to feel stuck.

One reason we resist the idea of accepting something we don't like is that we may feel as though we have conceded to a bully, and that bully chose for us when we had no say. If that is the way acceptance is seen, I can fully understand rejecting the idea. But acceptance has nothing to do with cowering before the ideas of someone else. If you've read my book *Jesus over Everything*, you know I am retired from what I call "the deadly overs." These are overdone behaviors, such as *over*apologizing, *over*explaining, and *over*analyzing (still working on this one), habits largely rooted in the need to please other people. Acceptance is not about that.

Acceptance is for you. Therefore, it is to your benefit. It is about not wasting your life pining over things you literally do not have the power to change, so your mind and heart can be free.

Many of us get stuck because we aren't willing to shift to things we can change and instead stay stubbornly convinced (for years!) that our willpower can work miracles. Acceptance is not giving up on something. It's making a decision to do what works. It's being courageous enough to move to something better: better fruit, better mental health, better perspective, a better life of hope and positivity.

Courage is also not a new idea, but one God Himself came up with many thousands of years ago. One of my favorite verses, the reference of which is tattooed in Hebrew on my son's arm: "Have I not commanded you? Be strong and courageous. Do not be afraid; do not be discouraged, for the LORD your God will be with you wherever you go" (Joshua 1:9). God gave this charge to Joshua in the wake of Moses' death, not to talk Joshua out of wishing Moses was still there to lead him. He gave it to help him accept the new call on his life to take the lead, even while he felt inadequate. Even as he missed Moses' leadership. Courage to overcome his fear. To move forward, even in a state of discouragement. To change his mind and heart and course of action. These were the things Joshua could actually change in the wake of those he could not.

Acceptance is about courage, not concession. When we are ready to take our life back from the what if, we will courageously accept the what is.

*Wisdom to know the difference.*

This may be the most crucial part of the serenity prayer: discerning between things we truly can't alter and those we can. Society tells us to approach our fate from one of two extremes, and both are incorrect. As with most things, secular culture tries to skew our focus in the direction of self rather than God, so it's no wonder things have gotten confusing.

- We must simply accept the cards we've been dealt and do nothing to improve ourselves or our situation.

    This approach goes along with the false and damaging humanistic "spiritual" narrative that God accepts us no matter what, and there is no spiritual standard or expectation that comes of a personal relationship with Him. Grace is an evergreen, no-strings-attached expectation. God just wants us to be happy; therefore, we can live however we want.

    If we believed this lie, many of our powerful testimonies

would be nulled: survivors of toxic home environments and abuse who worked to become great parents, for instance, or those without good resources who managed to become accomplished job holders. We are not victims to what we were born into. We may not control how we come into the world or, often, what happens to us, but we do have an absolute measure of control over what we do next. This is the beauty of free will and speaks to the possibility of new life with Christ. The odds may be against us, the road may be unclear and even obscured, but God can work miracles with our story.

- We are the masters of our own destiny; therefore, we must take all matters into our own hands and hustle our way through life.

By now we know how hustle culture has all but destroyed us. Hustle and hard work are two different things, and much of the time we have chosen the frenzy and self-reliance of hustle. The pandemic of 2020 yet again (and maybe even in a new way) taught us how much we resist rest, despite saying it's what we want. If we had anything when the world shut down for a while, it was more time, less travel, less opportunity to hustle. And it drove most of us crazy.

If nothing else, this proved that our reasons for not slowing down haven't really been about having more time; they've been about not wanting to slow down for one reason or another. For many of us, the pandemic gave us the out, and we fought it all the way. *Bring back our life and normalcy*, we demanded . . . after one week of enjoying an excuse for a slower pace. Maybe hustle has been a scapegoat for us not having to face the hard things. In the past we felt confident that "being too busy" was a safe and accepted reason for all manner of situations we didn't want to deal with. We gave it to people so they wouldn't question or press. And our payoff: we got out of having to work through complicating issues.

Believing everything is up to us, that we can indeed change, create, and control our life circumstances, renders God unnecessary. On the other hand, working hard can coexist with trusting God. We can strike a balance between acceptance (trusting God) and pursuit (working hard) when we invite God, and only when we invite God, to help us live within this tension. He helps us learn to accept the things beyond our control and deal with them so we approach our work and life in a healthy manner. This is godly balance, which brings serenity from the inside out, not the other way around. While the world preaches production, in order to become secure, we who have tried it that way know a well soul is the real producer. The world can't touch the peace of God protected by the walls of a settled heart.

The serenity prayer claims wisdom will be the decider between knowing what things we can and can't change. Wisdom and knowledge are different, as you may know. The wisdom of God is more than gaining information. It is discerning information under supernatural leadership and behaving accordingly. This means complete reliance upon the Holy Spirit, who is within us and leading us as our guide.

It is hard to accept things we wish were different. But it is good because the result is a surrender that allows our life to become unbridled. Believers in Jesus understand this process differently than the world. The world will tell us to simply *live unbridled*. That sounds great, but it's not possible without God because our sinful choices will eventually put us in chains once again. We consecrate ourselves to God, and in that we gain freedom. Remember: Godly acceptance isn't settling. It is becoming settled by letting Him lead our heart.

I've lived both ways—rebellious and surrendered—and I can

testify that the places God has asked me to lie down were for the good of my soul.

Acceptance has set me free to do things I otherwise could not. To create. To dream. To love. And to grow. And honestly? To get up in the morning.

Acceptance is how I came to love and enjoy a man named John, a man I now call my bonus dad and have grown especially fond of teasing and going on rattlesnake hunts with.

Acceptance is how I learned to become me, rising in my gifts and strengths while remaining utterly hopeless without God to help me with my weaknesses.

Acceptance is how I stopped restricting my eating as I did for so many years in college and even after.

Acceptance is how I moved on to enjoy a precious relationship with my father, even after mentally agonizing days and months over whether he'd had an affair and, in turn, harmfully acting out against myself. Accepting the fact that I might never know what actually happened and whether the affair story was true completely turned my life around.

Sometimes we wish for a baby, and we don't get pregnant, and we never know why.

Sometimes we lose someone we love, and it makes no sense. Even if we could make some sense out of it, the loss still feels unjust.

Sometimes we lose a job for no good reason.

Sometimes we want to get married, and it doesn't happen or at least not yet, and we feel unlovable, unheard, and unseen by the God we keep asking for it. Or sometimes we get married, and it doesn't work out the way we want.

Surrendering that need to know is hard, but it is powerful. If we want our minds to become free, this is how that happens.

Hard good is holy payoff.

And if I could say just one last thing? We so often want the benefit of a seasoned life without the seasoning. But life doesn't work that way. To live in acceptance means to live with the understanding that, at the end of it all, even the hard things will have been for our good. Then and only then can you and I repeat the words of that often-quoted saying: "A lot of things broke my heart but fixed my vision."

We are profoundly changed when we don't let the hard harden us but become goldened by its fire.

# CHAPTER 2

# cheering for someone when they get what you want

When someone else's happiness is
your happiness, that is love.
—Lana Del Rey[1]

I LIVE IN A HOME OF ATHLETES, RAISED IN THE SCHOOL OF HARD work and dedication—literal blood, sweat, and tears. When your boys play football and you're the mother who supports them, you learn early on to live with both the smells of their jerseys and the fears that require prayers for God to have them out there on the field. I expected sports to teach my kids important things. What I didn't expect is how much my children's experience with them would also teach me.

My boys never asked my permission to fall in love with football, or I probably would have said no. But my joy had no choice but to get on board, watching my sons do what they loved. My middle son,

Micah, started playing especially early, at the age of seven, for the local rec league at the nudge of the coach (a close family friend) and upon the lure of a fancy stitched uniform. He played receiver, and his best friend played quarterback. Every Saturday we loaded up the Suburban with coolers, donned T-shirts with "Whittle" across the back, and watched our boy play his guts out, often up against boys twice his size. When he scored his first touchdown, and then a second and a third in the same game, we knew his talent was going to take us for a fun ride.

Season after season, summer after summer of practice and off-season workouts, we lived through eleven years of football life. Getting up at six in the morning for workouts with the older boys, just to be near the sport, rec league to middle school to JV to varsity. Micah even had a summer stint as a volunteer coach's assistant when he was about ten and between seasons. When he was in eighth grade, he moved to a school ranked nationally in football. He was on a team of able peers; they all soared in the sport. As early as ninth grade, conversations in the stands began circulating about who might get offers to play at the next level, though the boys were barely fourteen.

Junior year of high school arrived, and with it, for hopeful athletes, prime season for college offers. Despite the team winning a state championship and despite Micah's hard work, the season was racked with personal disappointment. One by one, Micah's best friends who had sweated on the field with him for years received offers from big schools to play college football. Micah received none.

I watched the whole thing, my heart breaking for him a little more every time. I watched him get bypassed, and I sensed the pain of being overlooked. But what I saw at the same time taught me an invaluable lesson: I saw Micah cheer for each of his friends even while his heart wanted what they got. I knew he hurt. As I had so many times through the years when he took the field, I prayed for him. But this time I prayed something different.

I prayed that in the quiet of his bedroom, alone with his thoughts, God would keep him from envy. That he would be comforted in his pain. That he would know God saw him, cared for him, and had a plan for him far beyond football. That even though this moment was hard, he would eventually discover, in some way, why it was good.

I knew at least in one way it already was: the invaluable lesson of cheering for someone who gets what you want shapes your character in ways always winning never can.

Through this, my son would become a better man.

That was the real prize worth getting.

Undoubtedly you have your own story that involves a moment when cheering for someone else didn't come easy. When someone gets what we have worked for or desperately want for ourselves, it is almost unthinkable to celebrate their gain. Maybe you are thinking about what someone else has that you want right now. If not, it might not take you long to recall something. We aren't typically short on desire.

The risk for any of us who watch others get the engagement ring we want . . . the work promotion . . . the attention online . . . the coveted position in life we feel we've worked equally hard for or (buckle up—here's the truth) feel we deserve more, and then deny that those feelings exist, is that it can build bitterness, not character. So I don't want us to deny that we want things, as Jesus followers are prone to do, like "good Christians." I want us to work through the very human feelings.

Sometimes we are a *front-end reactor*. We take someone else's success hard right at first, but we pray, work through it, and wind up with a healthy perspective.

Other times we are a *back-end reactor*. We offer support

immediately, but later come to the realization of a perceived injustice, and we wind up angry. This way of processing often happens when a root of bitterness sets in (we will talk more about this later) and the good initial right attitude is derailed by negative thoughts that have festered over time. (Or at times the initial support wasn't sincere.)

Sometimes we never accept someone else's success or gain, never change our perspective to see any positive in it, and never let it change us for the good. Sadly, this is where a lot of us live, stewing for years over something someone else has that we never got. Something we may even still think we want that is clearly not meant for us.

The person who learns to cheer for someone else doesn't have those mental restraints, which is why they become such a usable force for the kingdom of God.

## The *E* Word (Entitlement)

One of our biggest roadblocks to cheering for other people is having a sense of entitlement. If that makes your eyes narrow a bit, I'm with you. But this is going to be big for you, so you'll like the breakthrough.

When Micah didn't get any offers for football, for a while all I wanted to talk to God about involved the word *fair*.

The entire family had sacrificed so much for him to have this opportunity to pay for his college education . . . monetarily, emotionally, and even spiritually with all those prayers. And (honesty alert) there was a part of me that felt as if God owed it to us to make this happen for my kid. After all, he was a good kid. We were good parents doing good things, like telling him to trust God. I am absolutely as put off by this as you are as I write it, but I'm committed to telling you the truth.

This me-centric attitude with God illustrates how we often operate in one of two unhealthy realms. We may go through life with an inflated sense of self, diminishing our sin. Or we might walk around under a cloud of guilt and shame, constantly racked by low self-esteem. Sometimes we toggle back and forth between them. But neither is more noble. Both put us on unstable footing.

When for most of our life we tend to be so inwardly focused, it's no wonder cheering for others becomes a notoriously hard task. In nearly every equation the thing we most need to shake off is *ourselves*. (This does not include being taken advantage of and boundary-less, which is not godly, has no merit, and stems from something completely different.) If this sounds foreign to your ears, it's probably because you've gotten used to the opposite message of this world that says *we* are the most important, which is fantastic to hear but not gospel. We actually aren't on the list when, in Matthew 22:36–39, God gives the top two Greatest Commandments: to love God (first) and love your neighbor (second), adding "as yourself" to give reinforcement to the depth perhaps because He well knows how much we love ourselves. Before you misunderstand this to mean that I don't believe we are important or don't believe in self-love, know that anytime God asks us to love others, it is with the sovereign understanding that on any level of its sacrifice, we will find our deepest fulfillment. This *is* a way to love ourselves.

When our flesh cries out for what other people have that we don't, we process some type of self-death. We're disappointed to death, embarrassed to death, or we're contending with the death of the dream of hearing a yes. *No*, after all, is a word we don't enjoy hearing.

Habits of self always go down swinging.

No, life isn't fair. But that's not exactly the problem.

The problem is we believe God owes us. Sure, we say, He has been good to us. But deep down we'd like Him to be better, to

*No, life isn't fair. But that's not exactly the problem. The problem is we believe God owes us.*

give us just this one more thing. Doesn't He see that we've done more to deserve it than the other person? In our private belief system, God is here to meet our needs, feed us with goodness and mercy, and bless us with riches and our idea of favor. When He doesn't come through, our flesh reacts like the Wicked Witch of the West being splashed with water. *I'm melting!* Who would want this?

Essentially we feel *entitled*. And when we have a mindset of entitlement, we devalue anything God might use to grow us up. Pain? Avoid it. Disappointment? Numb it. Refinement? Refuse it. Hard-good things to help us grow? Deny them. In short, avoid any bumpy, imperfect road.

Entitlement blocks us from cheering for one another. And yet, Scripture makes it clear we are to "rejoice with those who rejoice" (Romans 12:15). Paul also wrote, "If one member is honored, all rejoice together" (1 Corinthians 12:26 ESV). This is no casual request. Not only is our unity on the line, but our personal spiritual growth is too. The pathway to truest fulfillment is being the man or woman God wants. Cheering for someone who has what you want is one of the hard-good ways to get there.

Entitlement is also a hindrance to God's ability to do His greatest work in and through us. His *purpose* for us doesn't depend on our willingness to face and confront those feelings that often lead to behaviors, but our *usability* does. In other words, we will be limited in how powerful for the kingdom of God we will be, based on how much we let God chisel us through facing the hard, which in turn produces the good. Did you catch this distinction? *Purpose and usability are two different things.* God's purpose for us cannot be altered and has been predetermined—all believers have the same one to "go and *make disciples* of all nations" (Matthew 28:19). But we can live below our potential and never see God do the work in and through us He wants to do.

This is important, so let me dive into it a bit further.

If you read the intro of the book (I hope you did because book intros are my favorite), you read about how two things are up to God and one thing is up to us: God anoints and appoints us. But we determine our level of usability. Consider the difference between the way David and Saul handled things. Both were anointed and appointed by God for kingship. Both were imperfect. But because of the way they responded to the tendencies of the flesh, they were used very differently.

Both accomplished some things.

But only David yielded his will, and as a result, only David ever truly became God's man.

David knew he was going to be king. But at the time, Saul still held the position. No doubt, under Saul's poor leadership, David must have felt he could do the job better. No question, he wanted Saul dethroned. But he respected God too much to interfere. We see this throughout the book of 1 Samuel. In chapter 24, Saul was right where David wanted him, vulnerably relieving himself in a cave. Yet David didn't take what even his own men told him he was entitled to. He chose not to end Saul's life and grab the throne that was rightfully his. The war he fought wasn't with Saul but against his own flesh. This is the truth about us as well—what we often think is a battle about another person, in a time of conflict, resentment, or whatever it may be, is actually a battle within our soul to do what God wants. David's behavior in this moment determined the kind of man God would be able to use for many years to come. He chose to face the hard and let God leverage it for good.

Often we act as though once God has given something to

someone else, He's fresh out of blessings for us. This is when we begin to resent. But the kingdom of God isn't a place of scarcity. His supply doesn't dwindle. He can give someone something beautiful and give you something different-beautiful at the same time.

*He can give someone something beautiful and give you something different-beautiful at the same time.*

So what are we really believing when our instinct is to scramble instead of relying on the security in the promises of God?

Remembering our fate was death until Jesus chose the abundance of life for us helps cure us of fighting so hard for our rights. That thought alone pretty much kicks entitlement issues in the teeth.

## The *J* Word (Jealousy)

Another roadblock to cheering for other people is good old-fashioned jealousy.

Again, we need look no further than Saul to see how self-preservation in the moment and unwillingness to do the hard-good thing result in underdeveloped character and a life God can't fully use. When natural feelings of jealousy toward David arose within Saul's heart, he gave in to them rather than giving them to the God who could help him deal with them the right way.

> David went everywhere that Saul sent him, and did well. Saul had him lead the men of war. And it was pleasing to all the people and to Saul's servants.
>
> When David returned from killing the Philistine, the women came out of all the cities of Israel, singing and dancing, to meet King Saul, playing songs of joy on timbrels. The

women sang as they played, and said, "Saul has killed his thousands, and David his ten thousands." Then Saul became very angry. This saying did not please him. He said, "They have given David honor for ten thousands, but for me only thousands. Now what more can he have but to be king?" And Saul was jealous and did not trust David from that day on. (1 Samuel 18:5–9 NLV)

Unwarranted jealous thoughts barrage all of us at times, making it difficult for us to cheer for the other person. That's real life. It's what we do next that determines who we become. Whenever we allow God to use the hard moment, we lift our own souls out of a pit of self-pity and despair. We have to consider who might Saul have become had he handed over these jealous feelings for David to God rather than continue to let them accompany him throughout his entire journey. He was a capable, anointed, and appointed leader who did things for God, but what more could he have done? And how much more does God want to do with us, but our inability to cheer for other people is hindering it?

It was interesting timing as I was writing about this while sitting at my desk this morning that an email popped into my inbox from a woman I didn't know.

Dear Lisa,

I feel I should confess that I am a little bit jealous of your life. It seems like a lot of fun to write books and travel around and speak for a living. I hope that doesn't upset you, but I had to say it. But what I'm really writing to say is that sometimes, when an influencer with a large platform says women shouldn't feel competitive and there's more than enough room for all of us to do the same thing, I think to myself, "Easy for them to say." And I wonder, did they never feel jealous when they were starting out? Or are they just superhuman and don't struggle like I do?

Oh boy. If "S" from Texas only knew. I am either the best person to answer this question or the worst, depending on how honest she wants her answer.

In one sense, she is exactly right. The subtle shaming that takes place over real, human jealous feelings, especially among Christian women, is rarely addressed. We are not supposed to feel *those ways*. Often, instead of talking through them, we are talked out of them. Temporarily, of course, since the root of the feelings doesn't get dealt with. Eventually they crop back up.

It's a problem in Christian leadership because it's a problem in the church. Honesty about struggles hasn't historically been the way we handle things—it's more like the last resort and often only when outed.

I have not been immune to this struggle. At one time, in fact, it was the leading reason I didn't want to write books anymore. My focus on other people's success threatened to pull me away from my calling. (Keep reading; I will tell you more.)

What we really need (and want, I believe) is to be mentored so we know what to do with these natural human reactions. We want to live free of jealousy and support one another, but many of us have been shamed about our feelings instead of told how to exchange them for a better way. This is yet another example of the church not knowing what to do with someone who needs discipleship or accountability. I love the church. But we can be too busy building self-promoting empires to deal with the grunt work of taking on needs such as this, and we're often too personally compromised as leaders to be willing to confront another leader with an unhealthy ego, much less face it in ourselves. What we also need is to be honest about it with each other. But it takes a lot of maturity to have that conversation. So instead of investing, we typically either pretend jealousy isn't a big problem or suggest it is easily eradicated by simply determining to no longer be competitive. But not dealing with it doesn't help any of us grow or get healthy.

The second part of my response to this email, however, centers on something a bit different. One place where things go sideways is in our perception of "arrival."

For many of us, our view of a person's success from the outside is problematic to begin with. We can't know the full scope of someone's journey. There may have been rivers of tears, a fortune in education, and piles of rejections behind that successful, smiling picture. No doubt they dealt with both hard work and setbacks. Unspoken and unseen pressures. Insecurities and hierarchies to be overcome. *Arriving* is sometimes lonely, and often not at all what it seems. This is why social media, especially, is a harmful measurement of success in controlled information, filters, likes, and follows.

The word *success* in and of itself is fluid, open to personal interpretation, and somewhat undefinable. When we think it's the end goal, we will likely be disappointed. Hollywood stars often report back from their homes in the hills through memoirs, and even some from an untimely death of overdose or suicide that speaks from the grave: "Turns out, it wasn't the life I imagined in my dreams."

Getting what we want will never be what we want if we aren't okay without it.

So I think we have to confront what, in our own minds, we consider true arrival. Jealousy blocks our ability to cheer for other people, but it also blocks us from being in a position to be successful ourselves.

> *Getting what we want will never be what we want if we aren't okay without it.*

## The *B* Word (Bitterness)

About six months after Micah was overlooked by college football recruiters, I noticed he was more sullen. Quiet. Less willing to engage with us. For some eighteen-year-olds, this might pass as normal. But not for my typically easygoing, warm, family-oriented kid. A late-night text to him voicing my concern quickly pinpointed the problem: though he had been quick to cheer for his teammates who got something he wanted, in the months that followed, feelings of hurt and disappointment had crept in. And now he was bitter. (Think back-end reactor.)

"You've got to get rid of this bitterness," I told him. "It will severely affect your life." He acknowledged I was right but admitted he struggled to know how. I could empathize. Bitterness is a clinger. It gets its claws into you and hangs on for dear life.

> *Bitterness is a clinger. It gets its claws into you and hangs on for dear life.*

When we don't deal with not getting what we want, resentment can take root. Please don't ignore it. It might be exactly why you have trouble cheering for other people, and it truly can destroy your life. The Bible gives us an example of what could happen when we allow resentment to grow unchecked.

Now Abel kept flocks, and Cain worked the soil. In the course of time Cain brought some of the fruits of the soil as an offering to the Lord. And Abel also brought an offering—fat portions from some of the firstborn of his flock. The Lord looked with favor on Abel and his offering, but on Cain and his offering he did not look with favor. So Cain was very angry, and his face was downcast.

Then the Lord said to Cain, "Why are you angry? Why

is your face downcast? If you do what is right, will you not be accepted? But if you do not do what is right, sin is crouching at your door; it desires to have you, but you must rule over it."

Now Cain said to his brother Abel, "Let's go out to the field." While they were in the field, Cain attacked his brother Abel and killed him. (Genesis 4:2–8)

Our stories don't end well when we let bitterness overtake our hearts. We turn into people we don't want to be, led by feelings we don't want to have, doing things we don't want to do.

The Bible doesn't say specifically, but I am confident believing that Cain didn't initially want to be a murderer. Who would? He surely didn't come into this world intending to end the life of his brother. Yet he killed Abel in his heart long before he killed him with his hands. Bitterness is powerful enough to take us down these roads, so it will absolutely kill your spirit of joy for another person.

> *Our stories don't end well when we let bitterness overtake our hearts. We turn into people we don't want to be, led by feelings we don't want to have, doing things we don't want to do.*

While bitterness affects our own spiritual life, many of our problems stem from things we feel God has bestowed on others instead of us. This often feels like a cruel and purposeful withholding. Since we are most disappointed with God, running to the opposite of bitterness to help us is always a good choice. Gratitude is the perfect antithesis. When we spend time remembering all we have and expressing thanks, we feel differently than when we focus on where we feel God hasn't come through. Cheering for someone who has what we want is like a gift card we give ourselves to more freely see our blessings, and, as a result, we're not so focused on what someone else has. It all comes full circle. Especially when accompanied by prayer, confession, and study of the Word, cheering for someone else is the way to break those bitterness chains. Most of us don't take the initiative, instead waiting to feel joy for the other person. But when we choose the joy, our feelings follow suit. First take a chance. Then see the change in you.

This is where the good begins.

## ꙮ GOOD: ꙮ
### Their *gain* will no longer be your *loss*.

---

*There is an unexpected plot twist to the hard practice of cheering for someone who gets what you want: you wind up winning more than the actual winner.*

---

I understand that this sounds more Pollyannaish than possible, but if you've ever had a death-to-self experience, you know it's true: it's euphoric to feel genuinely happy for someone else.

It also has noticeable benefits in both your ability to produce and gain respect from others. When you cheer for someone who has something you want, it makes you:

- **RISE** in the lifting of others. People begin to notice a person with the ability to cheer for someone else.
- **SHINE** in the spotlighting of someone else. As you begin to elevate another person, you actually become elevated in other people's eyes.

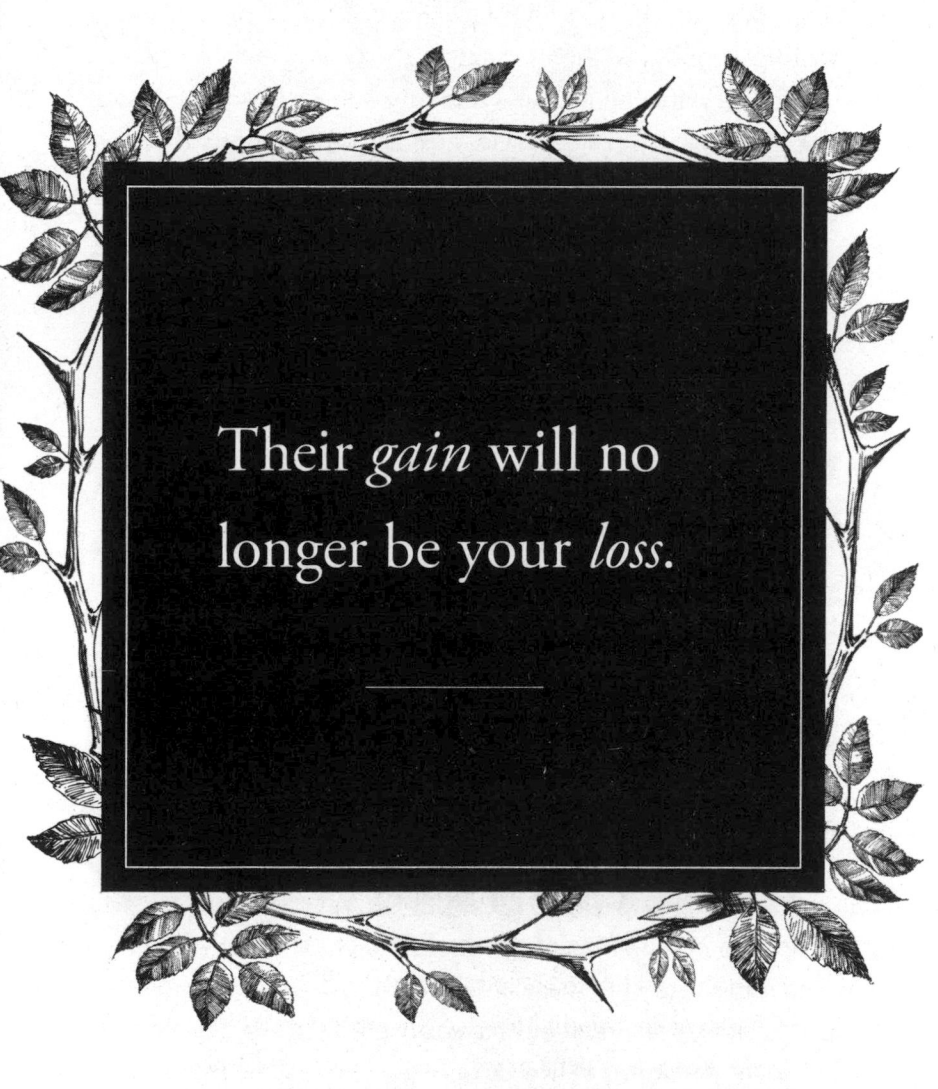

Their *gain* will no longer be your *loss*.

- **AND GROW** in the promoting of another. Supporting someone else creates openness, generosity, and freedom—things
  that spark more creativity because your heart is joyful, not
  jealous.

I'll tell you something else that may sound silly—it could save
you some money you'd otherwise spend on some therapy. When we
choose to cheer for someone else, we save ourselves from years spent
healing from wounds of resentment—wounds we would otherwise
gather on a train of envious feelings run amuck before we can stop
ourselves.

I'm about to give you a huge head start and potentially the
best little-known secret about how to kill the jealousy in your
heart: the minute you start to feel jealous of someone, take the
beast on.

I did this with my friend Kel.

She wasn't my friend, at first. I met her several years ago when
we were both on the docket to speak at a weekend conference. I
had never heard of her, so before I flew in, I visited her website
and could tell immediately she was a talented speaker. Even while
I looked forward to meeting a new ministry comrade and making
a new friend, my competitive nature kicked in. I wanted to do an
incredible job speaking, to match what I was certain was going to
be a phenomenal message from this woman.

The opening night of the conference arrived. We huddled up
as a team for prayer with a slew of volunteers in matching T-shirts,
the conference coordinators, musicians, and Kel. She would be up
first. Immediately I felt her charisma. Having been raised in a house
with a father who oozed it, I recognized it right away. Everyone in
the room was drawn to her, including me. Inside, my heart began
to battle. I didn't like her. I didn't want to like her. Everyone else
seemed to like her too much.

*She is too loud*, I thought to myself. *She's showy. She's not my style.* Even if these things were true (they weren't), the ugliest truth was this: I was jealous. My heart just didn't want to admit it. Lisa, the Bible teacher, the leader who was there to preach to women about how to be set free, stood in bondage to jealousy. The reality was jarringly painful.

"Let's pray!" the coordinator said enthusiastically, quickly breaking up my thoughts. As we bowed our heads, the Lord spoke to my heart. *Go pray over her, Lisa. Pray the power of the Holy Spirit over her message. Pray tonight, like you've never prayed before, for an anointing over this woman.*

There was no part of me that wanted to do that.

I knew what the power of the Holy Spirit could do with a gifted communicator. And I didn't want her to have that kind of power. I didn't want to have to follow behind what I was sure would be an incredible message from an incredible speaker *with the power of the Holy Spirit speaking through her.* No thank you—no way.

Had I waited ten seconds longer, those thoughts would have surely drowned out the voice of God. But for some reason, my legs started walking toward this woman I did not know, who had not spoken a word to me and was currently across the room praying her guts out.

Did I mention I'm a raging introvert, not someone who likes meeting new people or calling attention to myself?

With a spiritual gravity drawing me, I rested my hands on her shoulders and began to pray as never before. I asked for the power of the Holy Spirit. I prayed for a fresh anointing. I prayed with everything I had for this sister in Christ who did not know me or ask for me to pray.

Kel preached that night and was every bit the amazing communicator I thought she would be. To this day I consider her one of the best speakers I've heard. But the best news? She and I became dear friends. She's become a kindred sister, and I love her with all my heart.

I tell you this story because it was a rare and victorious moment when I took on jealousy before it overtook me. And I want you to know, firsthand, that this method works.

Too many times I've been envious of someone, and I've let jealousy fester and grow to the point it became a wildfire and incinerated any chance of relationship. They have had what I wanted, and my jealous feelings were blocking me from cheering for them. Conversely, I've lost out on relationships with those whom I have sensed let their jealousy get in the way of enjoying my friendship. It doesn't have to be this way. The body of Christ could use some renegades who decide we've had enough of allowing Satan to convince us the power of God is not enough to turn our jealousy into friendship.

Is it hard to cheer for those we envy? Yes. But it is far harder when we let the opportunity for healing go by and stay a person who is bitter and critical, year after year. The minute you begin to sense that jealousy rising in your bones, take it on. Walk over to the person you envy. Smile and embrace them with a hug. Show interest by asking a question. Engage. It's hard to resent someone you have touched. But it's easy to dislike someone from a mile across the room. That is why Satan works to keep us apart.

When you feel jealous, don't hesitate. Pray. For them and for you. As you take a step forward, deliverance is swift. This is where your once perceived loss will begin to feel like a gain, and where you once felt less than or powerless, you will begin to feel empowered. A huge win, right?

---

∞

---

## When You Withhold from Them, You Withhold from You

Cheering for someone costs you nothing. Withholding happiness from someone *costs you the health of your soul.*

A person who has never been genuinely happy for someone else is a miserable person.

This is the truth about the road to our greatest usability even through something like support of someone else's success: most of life isn't about getting better things. It is about becoming a better person. In that spiritual transformation process, we get the *greatest* thing, which is to be used by God for the kingdom of God.

It's still hard to wrap our brains around that being enough because we also want to get all the tangible things.

Most rewards on earth seem to be physical proof we did it all right. Houses and cars and vacations and money say we worked harder or smarter. Beauty, though often we had nothing much to do with it, says we learned the secret of looking good. We will say we value who we become in the process of living, but it doesn't always show in our system of rewards. A lot of the best people die unknown. It's hard to bear the thought of spending our lives denying ourselves and having to wait until the next life to gain rewards when we actually don't know what those rewards are. But this is a requirement of spiritual growth. When we withhold support from one another, we withhold our own benefits.

I can't deny that when we cheer for the one who gets the new house, the adoption placement, or the book contract, in that moment we may feel as though we are dying inside. It is hard because it is sacrificial—and sacrifice is not our norm. Most of us aren't used to denying ourselves. But this type of sacrifice isn't about unlearning self-care, neglecting rest, or dropping important relational boundaries. (Here's where self-first messages often go wrong, lumping everything into one category and encouraging us to choose self above all else.) This type of sacrifice is about choosing to honor others as we've chosen to honor God. And in the process, we watch Him use us for the good.

Nurturing the ability to usher in joy for our friends for their joy, even if the celebration falls during a time of our lack, is especially difficult. And yet it is where exponential growth occurs. The harder the ask, the greater work God does in us.

## The *L* Word (Love)

There is no higher desire in a human heart than the longing to be free, and in this case I mean literally.

So when I think about Paul writing four of his thirteen letters from prison, I marvel at his ability to be clear of mind, direct, and full of hope and gratitude. Read Ephesians, Philippians, Colossians, or Philemon, and you'll see what I mean. We don't find a pity party in these pages. We find strength, confidence, and an enviable experience of the presence of God.

But what is even more notable, perhaps, is Paul's overt cheering. Not only was he not bitter toward those outside the prison walls, but he constantly encouraged them, offering prayers of grace and peace, and reminding them that God was for them and so was he. With loving words penned from prison, he *served* them.

> I thank my God every time I remember you. In all my prayers for all of you, I always pray with joy because of your partnership in the gospel from the first day until now, being confident of this, that he who began a good work in you will carry it on to completion until the day of Christ Jesus.
>
> It is right for me to feel this way about all of you, since I have

you in my heart and, whether I am in chains or defending and confirming the gospel, all of you share in God's grace with me. God can testify how I long for all of you with the affection of Christ Jesus.

And this is my prayer: that your love may abound more and more in knowledge and depth of insight, so that you may be able to discern what is best and may be pure and blameless for the day of Christ, filled with the fruit of righteousness that comes through Jesus Christ—to the glory and praise of God. (Philippians 1:3–11)

This letter to the believers at Philippi wasn't an isolated event. Paul's signature style became one of constant lifting up, even while facing dire circumstances. In every way that mattered, Paul saw himself as a free man.

Did he want the freedoms enjoyed by those he was encouraging? Undoubtedly. Being bound in prison must have been excruciating for someone so passionate about spreading the word about Jesus.

But did his natural human desire to be free prevent him from desiring the good of his brothers and sisters in Christ? Absolutely not. Paul's lack didn't stop him from pouring out his surplus of wisdom from the Lord to help the body of Christ, knowing their gain meant ultimate gain for all. Imprisonment did not quash his cheering. It did not keep him from rejoicing in the Lord with those on the other side. There are three important things we can learn from this.

1.  Every win can become our win.

    When we understand the corporate purpose for which Jesus died, every win for the kingdom of God becomes our win. We see any gains in the gospel as our own, even when they aren't credited to us on earth. What a powerful, unifying mentality!

2. Every loss should become our loss.

Competition in the kingdom should become offensive and be seen as a loss. Breaking other believers down needs to be seen as a corporate mark. Paul modeled this mentality. It was learned through a burning love for Jesus—and the furthering of the gospel—and then funneled down to people, which is the way it will also work for us.

3. Love doesn't come naturally to us.

This might be something we've not recognized before, but surely our volatile behavior on the internet and to strangers who disagree with our points of view has proven the point. Perhaps the biggest reason we struggle so much to cheer for others is because we have tried to first force people-love without the help of God. Cheering for others won't happen without that core Jesus-love. We just aren't that altruistic. We can rejoice with people in our lack only out of the abundance of love God has lavished on us, and when we find that, alone, to be enough.

We have it in us to cheer for another person—we have *God in our bones*. This is a beautiful thought. Let Him seep out of your mouth, your smile, your very pores when someone gets blessed or honored. You are fully loved by God, and out of that fullness you can feel joy in the gain of another.

Did you get that? *Feel joy in the gain of another.* This is next-level from simple acceptance of another's gain. What if more of us came to this healthy place? How might it look in the body of Christ? Perhaps we would be more aligned with the early church model we see in Acts 2—the one we always look to emulate in the church.

They devoted themselves to the apostles' teaching and to fellowship, to the breaking of bread and to prayer. Everyone was filled with awe at the many wonders and signs performed by the apostles. All the believers were together and had everything in common. They sold property and possessions to give to anyone who had need. Every day they continued to meet together in the temple courts. They broke bread in their homes and ate together with glad and sincere hearts, praising God and enjoying the favor of all the people. And the Lord added to their number daily those who were being saved. (vv. 42–47)

Note the health and maturity of these early believers' hearts.

- Talents and gifts were cheered by all.
- Abundance was shared by all.
- No one was jealous of what anyone else had.

The result was powerful kingdom growth.

As you and I "encourage one another and build each other up," we take on the tone of the early church (1 Thessalonians 5:11). And when we flip the script on our definition of church, we will watch the church change. Home church. Megachurch. Small, intimate congregation. These are all simply preferences. For too long we've focused on church structure. But issues of the heart aren't solved by more square footage, better light fixtures, or worship style.

Jesus doesn't care about the stats or the aesthetics. He cares about why we do what we do.

We *can* change. I want us to change—to be honest, grow, and deal with character issues like this with better discipleship, starting with our leaders. *I want to change.* I want to cheer louder for people in the coming years of my life than I ever have before, even when it's hard. The hard good of this seemingly lesser hard of life cannot be missed because its impact on who you become is monumental.

*Jesus doesn't care about the stats or the aesthetics. He cares about why we do what we do.*

The heart issues that die hardest in us are often the quieter, nagging places God has been speaking to us about the longest but we have ignored. How long have you been privately struggling to cheer for others? Take on that history and start a new one today.

Entitlement, jealousy, and bitterness can all be part of your past. Love, in which their win is your win, can be a part of your future.

Cheering for others is possible:

*It will change you for the better.*
It will keep bitterness from breaking you down.
It will honor God, who will honor you back.

If this feels hard to you, today, please remember: the harder road leads to the better human.

# CHAPTER 3

# showing up when you want to shut down

The cost of a thing is the amount of what I will call life, which is required to be exchanged for it, immediately or in the long run.
—Henry David Thoreau[1]

I never expected John to come out of the house wearing Dad's cowboy hat.

It was the summer after Dad died, during John's first official visit to our beautiful state of North Carolina and a trip to the lake. Every new guest gets the offer of an outing on the boat if the time of year is right, but this time I had wished for the impossible: that John might somehow know my history with and love for lakes without me having to fill him in. Maybe then he could better understand why I wanted him to feel so honored to be asked on this sacred outing.

Lake Norman, a stunning, almost thirty-four-mile-long man-made lake, had been our family's church on the water while the kids grew up—the place we found community with one another and peace from hard weeks. The perfect Carolina blue sky backdrop, glistening water, and beautiful homes nestled in stately trees were just a few of the reasons it felt like our favorite place on earth. Even boat trouble was sacred in a way, and we had plenty of it. Every moment of fun made up for the problems when that familiar hum of the boat played in the background like a family movie soundtrack as we cruised on the rippling lake. This is where we'd brought our babies since they were newborns, and magically, that first rock of the water lulled even my most stubborn boy fast asleep. They all witnessed at least one bad storm, at least one snake, and at least a half-dozen fights between their parents. I'm not proud of that part. But as calming as the lake was for us as a family, it couldn't always calm our feisty marriage back in those days.

We all grew up on that lake. But that wasn't all. The lake held stories about my dad.

"They will have pretty babies someday," he once said to my future mother-in-law during a ride around Lake Norman to celebrate our new engagement with both sides of the family, Scott's and mine. Daddy was right. Thanks be to God, we sure did.

But my tenderness wasn't about Lake Norman in particular. It was mostly about the remembrance of water, lake memories in general, and my favorite person. That triad held years of my childhood, and it involved yet another lake near where we lived at the time in Oklahoma, Lake Tenkiller, which we frequented. I can still see my father there, standing in the water, smiling widely, his dark hair full of suds from washing in the lake. "C'mon, Lisagirl," he would call for me to join him (I always would) . . . and the two unconventional besties would enjoy a good hair cleaning *our way* for just a bit. It was just one of the dearly beloved traditions I looked forward to every summer, along with campfire smells and night fishing for bass. You must know: I didn't care a thing about the fish. I just wanted to be near Daddy. Even if it meant sleeping with my face pressed against the synthetic carpet in the bottom of a hard boat.

But John couldn't possibly know all this.

And now, at my request, he had come to visit my mother during their season of long-distance dating, as I felt a man properly courting a woman should. I had promised my father I would take care of my mother after he died. It is exactly what I intended to do, though I was second-guessing my choice to invite John into such a personal aspect of our lives. I wanted to involve him in our favorite activity, but I also didn't want to share with him this intimate space so soon.

Knowing what our day trip to the lake held, I had prayed for a welcoming attitude, excitement to show John our traditions, and no emotional breakdown. I knew those things would be necessary for it to go well. On our way there, Scott and I and the kids swung by Mom's house to pick up Mom and John. Mom was the first one out of the house, with John following closely behind. At first I couldn't make out the details of what he was wearing on his head. But then Mom moved out of the way. John moved closer to the car. And I saw it.

*Dad's cowboy hat.* His light one, with the small black band all the way around. The one he'd bought after it caught his eye with that exquisite taste he had. The hat he had sweated in. The one he wore in all the happy pictures as Papa, with his arms wrapped proudly around my kids. The one that said *Jim* in every way—the hat that fit his head *when he was alive.* Jim's hat, not John's.

It's funny how a little thing can become everything in a matter of a few seconds.

Everything inside me begged me to break down right there on the spot. To rip the cowboy hat off John's head and tell him he was insensitive at best for wearing my dad's hat, and cruel, at worst. *You will never be him*, I wanted to say. *You cannot wear anything of his. Are you oblivious?* To make matters worse, John seemed to notice nothing out of the ordinary, nor did Mom. How could this not make their short list of things that might bother me right now?

In the previous months, I'd become accustomed to the unwelcome visitor of tears, as well as the difficult, sweet ironies that often popped up when it came to Mom and John. He often told the same preacher jokes as Dad. Wore similar eel-skin cowboy boots. Used the same hunting lingo. Mom responded to him in the same playful, gracious way she always had with my father, serving him tea at his request and bragging about his preaching. I knew God had ordained this divine connection. No one else could have made something like this up.

But knowing something is right doesn't always make it less hard in the moment. It still hurts. I've been learning, through these and other similar moments, that we can get through hard things when we know God is in them. What is spiritually right, even though it's unwanted, is good—because it is who God is and, thus, will be to our benefit in some way. But at the moment, we don't want to hear this. We just want relief. And in order for our emotions not to overtake our understanding, we need God more than ever to make it through the immediate pain and to process it in the long term.

*I need You, God,* I said silently in my seat. *I can't do today without You.* I meant every word. Jesus was the only One who could help me get through it. I needed Him like I needed my own breath. The threat of a shutdown was imminent and real. I had been triggered by a cowboy hat, but an avalanche of unwelcome thoughts and emotions came next. It was wrong to enjoy the day. It wasn't fair to be on the boat where Daddy once rode while he lay in a grave. Suddenly everything we had planned for our lake outing with John seemed ridiculous and wrong. I wanted to lash out at him and Mom for everything and nothing and mostly just run away.

Emotions can be a very strict boss. But I wanted more than just to get by. I needed more than just not to shut down. I needed to show up—for Mom, for John, for the other family members who had come to enjoy a day at the lake. For *me*.

Have you ever wanted to be better than that loud outburst or sulking in the corner, but you always wind up there? It feels awful thirty minutes later when you can't take anything back, and you're tired of that feeling. You want to be that person they call the bigger person when someone triggers you *yet again*, but you have never quite seemed to find her inside yourself. Welcome to a lot of us.

Emotions might be bossy, but they are also a consistent truth teller. This is an excellent quality because we need to know where the trip wires are inside our soul to learn how to defuse them. Shutting down often involves shutting *out* people. This is obviously bad on relationships, and it also never makes us happy in the end—to feel overcome by our reactions rather than having handled them.

The first thing, then, is to begin to recognize when we are shutting down and what triggers it, and work on not giving in to that anymore. We'll talk more about the signals of a shutdown in a minute, but most of us know ourselves enough to recognize the signs when we are about to close off. One-word answers. Looking off or picking up our phone. Interrupting someone. Eyes brimming with tears. Getting hot all of a sudden. A snippy comment. Not participating in something we otherwise would. When we sense these things happening, we have to act fast with an alternative action. Deep breath. Mentally counting to twenty. Quick silent prayer to God (think "it's time to send up the SOS"). And even stepping out to get some fresh air if you're inside. We aren't a victim to the shutdown, which is great news if you have historically struggled with staying open. Is it hard to stay open? It can be. But shutting down leaves us in a cycle of regret and inability for God to fully use us.

Then we replace shutting down with showing up. This is

next-level health, especially when it is done to combat the pull to shut down. (It is the best way, in fact.) Then you are truly taking back power from your emotions. Sometimes we show up even when we don't feel it or feel we can. (Different from setting necessary boundaries in some cases—again, the wisdom to know that difference from chapter 1's serenity prayer is a crucial Holy Spirit need.) That funeral we never wanted to go to . . . that family gathering we swore we wouldn't set foot in . . . that church we walked back in after never again wanting to walk back in . . . yes, we can show up when everything within us doesn't feel it.

So don't wait on a sign. Your sign is that you are tired of feeling numb or embarrassed or regretful over shutting down, yet again. Your sign is you want to fully experience life. You long to be a more open person. You want to be truly *okay*. But showing up means more than hanging on, more than mere survival, which a lot of us do year after year. It requires being fully present. Showing up is a way to defy death—not literal death, but the kind that happens before we know it, while we are still alive. When loved ones die, they gift you with something, if you choose to receive it. A fresh desire to be present for your life. It is as if they breathe back into you one more chance to appreciate the life they no longer get to have. I feel this. Since the moment Dad died, settling has become a less attractive option.

> *Showing up is a way to defy death—not literal death, but the kind that happens before we know it, while we are still alive.*

Pay close attention to this gift, by the way, when it comes. It won't come with fanfare. Instead, you may find yourself willing to learn new things for once. Or checking things off the to-do list. Or saying things, like life is short, which you already knew, but now you actually know it.

We don't need grief or loss to teach us that. But often our disappointments and dark valleys are the best teachers.

In case you're still thinking or wondering about the lake story: John wore Daddy's hat the whole day. All the way to the lake. Every minute as we toured him around Lake Norman on the boat, like good tour guides. While eating at the restaurant. All the way home and to the final goodnight. And I watched him in it. And him with Mom. And us on the lake without my first and favorite lake buddy.

And God held me together. It was hard, and it was good.

For many hours, under a perfect Carolina blue sky, we ate, laughed, told stories, and watched John, with a twinkle in his eye, fall in love with our family lake.

Did I mention John loves water too?

And after a long full day, I went home and cried myself to sleep.

It *is* possible: you can honor your emotions but not let them shut you down and steal another moment of joy from your life.

## For the Person Who Wants to Shut Down Right Now

Satan has a very vested interest in shutting you down. The more you shut down, the less you will do for God.

You know things are desperate—even for an introverted woman—when you loathe the idea of showing up for a fresh color and cut. But that's how far down the rabbit hole I had gone in 2002, after my husband, Scott, lost his job. I was mothering three children under the age of four, nursing the needs of an out-of-work husband, and desperately shutting down by the weight of it.

I dreaded showing up for my hair appointment only to have my nosy stylist ask me questions: How was I doing? How were the kids? Been to any good restaurants in town lately? I'd never thought of her as nosy before, only conversational. But that was *before*. Before we'd gotten a swift kick in the teeth by life. Before we didn't know what was next. Before we had to pull the kids out of preschool and put our house on the market. Before life wasn't as good as it had been when I didn't even realize how good it was. Suddenly my life was split into two lives—the *before* and the *after*—and I saw everything through that lens.

At this point I didn't want to show up for my kids. Or for church. Or for lunch dates with friends. And I sure didn't want to show up for sex with my husband, as mentally and physically exhausted as I was.

I didn't want to show up for my life. Ineffectiveness often starts with weariness left unaddressed. Before we know it, lack of sleep becomes problems melatonin can't solve.

*How do I parent these kids when I can't even take care of myself?* This was real. Even my hygiene was suffering. Turns out, when you are parenting three tiny babes, if they are going to be okay, it's impossible not to show up, at least in some physical form. I'd tried—venturing out a few times with friends for a long-overdue girls' night out—and it wasn't pretty. My husband is good at many things, but wrangling three toddlers was not one. I knew that no matter how I was feeling, somehow I had to keep showing up.

But my body fought me, physically, at every turn. So did my mind, which was the most formidable fighter of all. It told me to run into the farthest forest, escape into the trees, and make my body as small as possible so when they sent out a search party, I couldn't be found. It told me to get into my car and drive somewhere and tell no one where I was going. It told me to search Facebook for old boyfriends I cared nothing about just to see what they were up to after all this time. It told me to watch hours of mind-numbing TV, even some of those channels I would typically avoid—the ones we hadn't paid for but that now *just happened to* show up for me to stumble across late at night. The battle was real.

And it assigned me other things to do that were more quietly damaging. It told me to decorate incessantly, never satisfied with the pillows or the lamps, which was a particularly bad idea in a time of lost income. Then it told me that dreaming about new paint colors and upgraded couches for my living room wasn't enough. I needed bigger dreams to keep me up all hours of the night. I needed to plan one more vacation, more exotic than the last. I needed to *just keep shopping*. In many ways those eighteen months catalyzed a "deadly over" of overindulgence and a growing consumeristic appetite.

Some of the things my mind told me to do, I did. And some I prayed away with the help of God. But all of them I considered. When your mind tells you to do certain seemingly innocuous things, you don't always recognize that it's a means of shutting down or shutting out the pain or the hard thing. That's Satan's bet: to get you to comply without much deep thought. If he can get you to accept a temptation at face value, you might call it a fun and harmless pastime instead of what it is. Before you know it, that harmless activity has its grip on you. It has become a habit. Then the Enemy casually moves on to the next vulnerable subject or your next vulnerable place.

This is why getting to know the way Satan works is crucial. It is also why we need to understand that he is, indeed, after our emotions. We need not ignore or fear our foe; we need to be aware of him and the sin traps we're likely to fall into. Many episodes of spiraling sin are caused by the hard thing we never reconciled but instead numbed away. This is why Jesus has to be priority—*over* our overindulging. This includes indulging our tendencies to run away instead of facing a hard thing because it is easier in the moment to do so. It might be easier. But it is never better, and it will never help us grow.

> *We need not ignore or fear our foe; we need to be aware of him.*

We don't *want* food to consume our thoughts or to become a slave to the gym. We just like working out a lot. It's not that we meant to become dependent on that glass of wine. We just liked it to take the edge off. These are just a few ways we avoid addressing core issues, and sometimes that can be confusing if it is a good thing, like exercise. That's where we need the Holy Spirit. He alerts us to good behavior gone excessive in an attempt to deflect from being present and fully awake in a life that isn't always easy.

These mentions might feel like an extreme leap, or maybe you are thinking, *Lisa, you have no idea what stories I could tell you.* I've yet to meet someone who didn't struggle silently and think they were the only one. We live in a world that fights gospel purity. It is hard to be a believer in Jesus in this time. And these places are where we often go. This is where it starts—and then one day we wake up and we've wound up somewhere else completely. Hard seasons do funny things to us. Strong people, good Christian people, people who know better—no one is immune to wanting to feel an escape. The pull to shut down is strong. That is why we have to continually practice showing up—body, mind, and soul—and asking Jesus to help us stop the numbing methods that stifle that good process.

I do not stand in any kind of judgment. Instead, I come with deep understanding for our human plight. Remember, I'm the one who just admitted I didn't want to show up for sex with my husband. You likely judge yourself for wanting to shut down. But don't let your self-judgment keep you from God or His grace. We need God to help us show up for our lives during hard times, more than ever. Pulling away now will only weaken us in the places we need to be made strong.

Life is almost always what we blame for how things go badly for us, but the truth is we choose most things and spend the rest of our lives living with our choices. What have been your numbing patterns in the past? In what way(s) are you showing up for your life right now? What might look different in your world if, moving forward, you choose not to shut down anymore, no matter how hard things get? I hope you'll ask yourself these questions, today, and really be honest.

*Pulling away now will only weaken us in the places we need to be made strong.*

Some of us haven't even considered that showing up for our life was a true option.

If you believe that God is strong, you must believe He is strong enough to help you begin to show up for your life . . . instead of once again reaching for the alcohol or the porn or the food. Even if you have a long history of shutting down. Even if you find yourself in a tough moment, tougher than the last, and the temptation is strong.

No one wants to do a great work in you more than He does.

## ಬ GOOD: ಲ
### Your bossy emotions will be conquered by the strength of managed feelings.

*Imagine being a strong, confident person.*

If you're not there right now, God can help you get there, I promise.

But He doesn't force it on you or do it for you. Just as He doesn't ask you to deny your feelings as though they are bad and you shouldn't have them.

To develop this strength and confidence (aka to be able to show up for your life, even in the midst of hard things), He asks that you listen to Him. Yes, that's initially it. There is a very specific way He uses to communicate to you, to show you where you are, and to guide you to begin to be someone who shows up for her life in a powerful new way. But you have to listen and pay attention.

Your body is key in this showing-up or shutting-down journey. That is the communication piece I'm talking about. It is wild to think about, and yet it makes perfect sense that the same vessel that shuts down is the same useful tool God uses to alert us when it's happening. In other words, *He uses what is hurting us to help us.* This is so often the process of God.

Everything in the hard-good realm is a matter of body, mind, and soul. It is the way God created us—a complete picture, not a compartmentalized human. If you are unsure, consider 1 Thessalonians 5:23: "Now may the God of peace himself sanctify you completely, and may your whole spirit and soul and body be kept blameless at the coming of our Lord Jesus Christ" (ESV). I love how God names our facets here, while reminding us of the full picture. We are whole beings, and our need for Him isn't one-dimensional. Our complexity hungers for the everyday input of its Creator. We need God to guide our minds, keep our hearts beating, and heal our souls. At the same time, in each of these areas, we bear responsibility for how we manage the goods.

In order to show up for our life, we must not ignore the signs that our emotions are taking over, and we need God to help us not to shut down. When we listen well, we are given insight into exactly where we need healing.

### 1. Don't ignore your body.

At this point you might have felt a small twinge because the body is a tender subject for you. You already know—it is for me too. But let me share my truth first. I spent many years ignoring one of the biggest spiritual components of myself and, in the process, compromising my relationship with the Lord. I don't want that for you. I also don't want you to mistake your wrestling in this area for something else. Often, we can't see how something like our lack of attention to the physical affects the spiritual, and this can be a crucial miss. A powerful part of showing up for our lives is a physical showing up.

On a very simplistic level, it's not hard to figure out that a Creator would have the desire for His creations to take care of themselves. First Corinthians 6:19–20 supports this when it says, "Do you not know that your bodies are temples of the Holy Spirit, who is in you, whom you have received from God? You are not your own; you were bought at a price. Therefore honor God with your bodies." With all my body struggles, I appreciate God making His intention simple for me.

As a parent, I think of it in terms of my own children, and if you are a parent, maybe you'll relate. It pains me to think of any of them getting an accidental cut or wound to that skin I've loved, bathed, and cared for (which happened plenty of times when they were growing up. I had football-playing boys, remember?)—much less if they were to have such a disregard for life that they ingested drugs into their bodies, cut themselves in an effort to ease their pain, or drank their liver to cirrhosis. Some of us as parents know the pain of watching our kids do these things. It is brutal to be a bystander. And God, with so much greater love and so much greater investment as the Creator, must feel such deep anguish over the way we recklessly treat our bodies too.

But it's not that there's only scriptural evidence—or even common sense—to support what I'm saying about our bodies giving us signals. Science backs it up as well; just look at our fight, flight, or freeze instinct, for instance, if we come face-to-face with a tiger. Studies have shown that this stress response is a reaction to protect ourselves, and it causes hormonal and physiological changes.[2] In other words, our bodies hold a lot of power. And they absolutely hold the power to shut us down.

What has your body been telling you about the thing that is hard for you? And has it been giving you an accurate picture? I'm not saying your body is lying to you—I would never disrespect it in that way. Our bodies are astute observers of our surroundings. They hold much wisdom. But they also want and need to be guided—just like our minds and hearts—by truth.

Sometimes a body may perceive that something is a tiger, and it's not a tiger at all. But we react as though it is because it's been listening to a mind that isn't giving the correct picture. This is why we have to ask God to help us get well, wholly. Every part of us affects some other part. We trust our bodies. But we trust them only when they are guided by God, not by human emotions.

In the same way, our bodies affect how mentally strong we can become. They can be a huge asset in doing intel for our steps to healing. Paying attention to what is happening in our bodies in a moment when we're tempted to shut down can be a game changer for discovering what lie we may be believing, what core truth we struggle to accept, or what trigger we're overlooking. Is our pulse racing and voice shaking? Are tears close or palms sweating? How's that blood pressure? Have we forgotten to breathe? Our bodies are taking a cue from our emotions and perceptions, and they're trying to tell us something. They may be screaming, *Pay attention to me! Focus here too. We all work together, and if you want to honor your life, you will do things—even little, seemingly insignificant things—to help you not shut down in this moment of pain.*

Like unclenching your jaw, for starters.

Little big things, right?

Your willingness to deal with hard things head-on, even when your body tells you to flee or shut down, reveals how much you value your life. Maybe you've convinced yourself that avoidance of difficulty, cloaked in choice, is self-preservation and self-care—a show of your being strong and in control. You might just call it liking to lie in bed and binge a good show on Netflix. Don't misunderstand—I love a good chill day. I need them at times, and you do too. So this could be listening to our bodies telling us to rest. But sometimes our choices become our entertainment therapists because they are easier than the alternative of facing the pain. Once we understand the correlation between facing hard things and meeting our potential, we won't love avoidance quite the same. It won't feel as safe to hide in a wobbly fortress.

If you're feeling as though this all just sounds good on paper, please don't forget you're hearing from someone who spent an entire day with a man wearing her father's favorite cowboy hat, fresh after her father's death. I know about triggers, unfair feelings, your body screaming at you—and making a choice. When the tsunami of feelings threatened to sweep over me that day, I struggled to keep my chin above water. I had to pray the waves down, knowing I couldn't myself stop them. It wasn't about pretending I was fine. That wouldn't have worked even if I had wanted it to. (I am a horrible actress.) It was about getting help from the Lord to control the body *He* had created, to help me keep my emotions in a wise, managed place, tethered to Him. He helped me lead my emotions and my body to a powerfully controlled place where I could show up for a day that was important to me, and, in the quiet of my room later, cry the feelings out.

Had I reacted as I wanted to, we would have had a ruined day,

> *Once we understand the correlation between facing hard things and meeting our potential, we won't love avoidance quite the same.*

and I might be apologizing for my behavior still. Let's just say the fleshly Lisa can get pretty fiery.

In those moments this is the real contest: Will we let God control us, body to mind to soul, or will we try to do it without Him? These moments are the deciders in life, crucial to whether we will show up or shut down. A chance to choose the hard good. Hard because—well, hello. Good because of how injustices (perceived and real), grief, and hard-fought humility keep our hearts and souls open as they must be to truly experience life and walk strong and confident.

No one wants to go through life feeling as if our emotions are managing us. When we show up in hard moments, we reverse this.

## 2. Don't ignore your mind.

My friend Kennesha asked me this question in an interview the other day: "Why do we struggle to admit we are weak or ask for help?" It was not one of our preplanned questions. But God meant for us to talk about it—that I know.

Even if you are not cut from the same cloth as Kennesha and I (no-nonsense women known for being the strong ones for everyone else), it is innate for many of us, due to our chronic self-reliance and pride, to not reach out in those times when we actually need someone. Sometimes we hold this up like a medal, all the way to a counselor's office, where the counselor has to help us unravel years of a stoic belief system that we don't need anyone and help us realize how much that medal has actually cost our soul. Other times we know our resistance to reaching out is not a good thing, and we long for a way to communicate to someone how much we do need help . . . or at least pray that our hints will finally be picked up.

But there's another reason many of us stay shut down—we don't let our guards down and reach out for help. In those times in the past when we did take the risk and asked for help, someone mismanaged our vulnerability. My theory is this is the "tough girl's" biggest secret: We are a society of broken hearts from mismanaged vulnerability. And because of that, we have vowed never to be weak again.

The reason this matters is if your mind tells you that it's not safe to be vulnerable, you'll never show up. Shutting down—aka isolating yourself—never letting down your guard and asking for help, and never admitting something is hard or that you are struggling will always be the comfortable place even when it is killing you. If you have been wounded and had your worst fear of betrayal confirmed, it feels better to hurt on your own terms than on the terms of someone else.

And it will take a painful undoing. Especially because of what happens next. Think of it as a domino effect that looks like this:

Belief → Hope → Risk → Breach → Lie → Belief

We have a belief that being vulnerable might be a bad idea. But we hope we are wrong, and we want to take that chance because we know we need to grow. So we take the risk, and it is terribly scary. Only to have someone mismanage our vulnerability by taking advantage of something we tell them and tell someone else, preying upon a weak area we admit to them and using it against us as a weapon in some way, or simply not honoring a tender place in our life by handing it back tenderly—which creates a breach.

Satan then jumps on the opportunity to shut us down, mentally and emotionally, by saying things to us like, *See! You should have never trusted anyone. You should stay on an island and never ask for help. Never ever do this again!* And just as he has whispered lies before to others, Satan adds just enough truth so the lies can be believed. So the belief system is now formed around lies, and the mind shuts down to the idea that we should show up, open up to people, and be vulnerable with them again.

Any of this ringing true?

In what way(s) has your mind been told something you have had a hard time getting past?

You might think this sounds as though I am encouraging a mental dismissal, but please don't hear that. To ignore the most powerful part of the showing-up versus shutting-down process—your mind—is to cause yourself great harm. In fact, I'd say that you won't ever be able to show up for your life and for the work God has for you until, with His help, you get your mind right.

This does not mean your mind will not struggle with lustful, anxious, depressing, perfectionistic, angry, and all other manner of sinful thoughts at times. It will. Our minds never stop being human, no matter how much counseling, prayer, and medication we seek. I've written extensively elsewhere—from free resources on my website to other books—about the importance of fortifying our minds. We can't stop Satan's attacks on our minds. But we can prevent them from taking over our hearts by filling our minds with the truth of the Word, stopping the intake of things that aren't good for us via our senses, and praying and asking for God's help. (Read Ephesians 6:10–18 for more about putting on the armor of God.)

So no matter what has happened to you in your past or what lie you've been told, know that your wellness depends upon your willingness to let God heal your mind.

A simple prayer right now is a great idea:

*Your wellness depends upon your willingness to let God heal your mind.*

*Jesus, only You and I know the ways my mind needs to be healed. Please heal that mind of mine You made as only You can. I want to show up for my life. I want You to use me. Amen.*

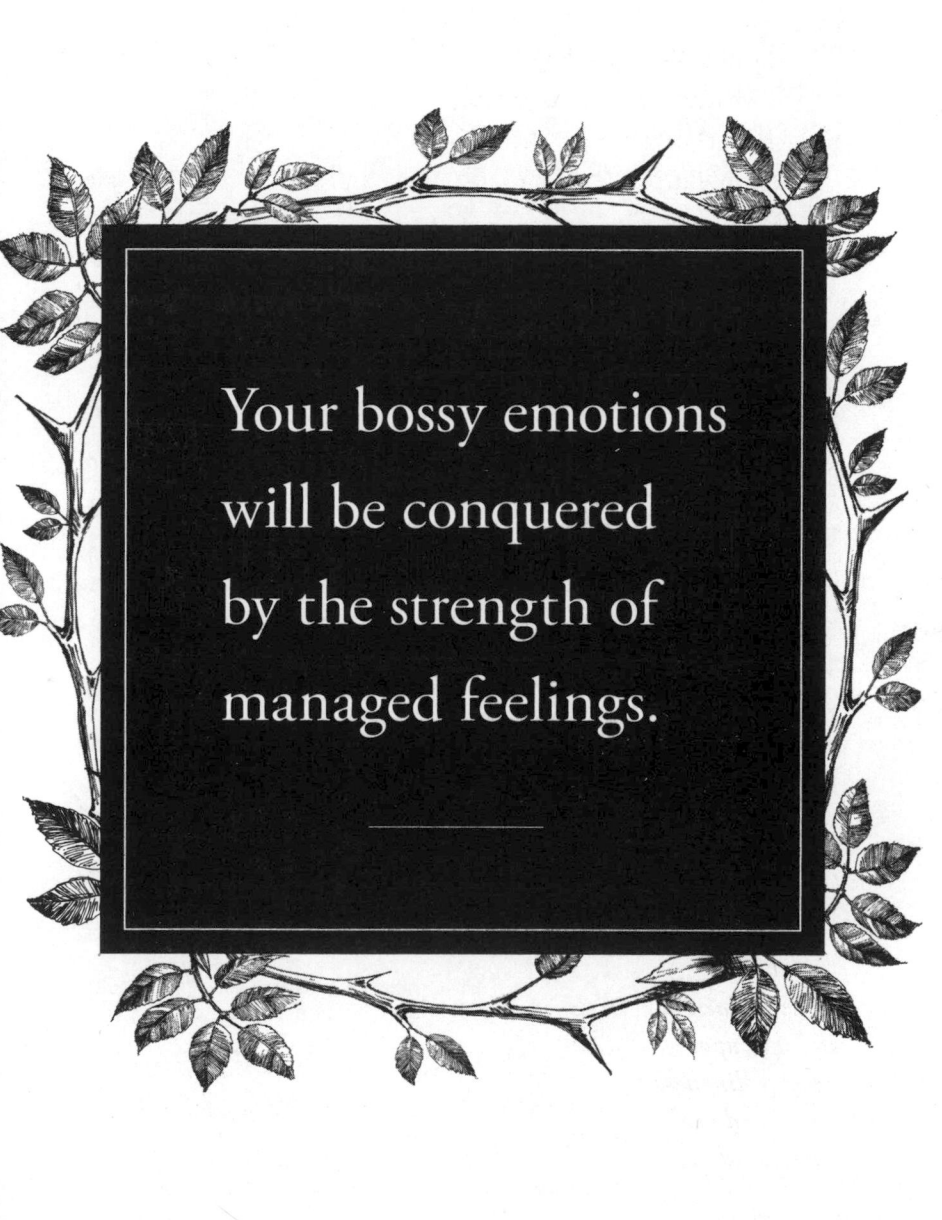

Your bossy emotions
will be conquered
by the strength of
managed feelings.

### 3. Don't ignore your soul.

A simple silver hook outside my shower taught me a lesson the other day: if a hook is not big enough, your towel will fall to the floor—every time. You probably already know this because you catch on much quicker than I do. I, however, learned this after five frustrating attempts to hang the same towel on the same hook and the subsequent falls to the floor seconds later. Since I love my towels and don't want smaller ones, my only solution is this: *find a bigger hook.*

In the midst of writing this chapter, the parallels were uncanny: there's not much that doesn't feel as if it's falling to the ground these days. If that is true, our *hook* will need to be adequate for these difficult times. Since problems aren't getting any smaller, the only solution is a hook big enough to handle what we put on it.

One thing I know: that hook sure can't be me. With how maxed-out I currently feel, if you try to hang one more thing on me, I'll surely drop it all on the ground. I am pretty sure you're not an adequate hook either. I think we know who the Hook is, and praise God for that.

The anchor verse of my last book, *Jesus over Everything,* is Colossians 1:17: "He is before all things, and in him all things hold together." Never has this verse meant as much to me as it does now. Many days, if I didn't believe He was holding all this together, I would have shut down. I can't show up for a life that just ends or ends in tragedy. I can't get excited or feel hopeful if it's all up to me. Someone has to be the Hook for my soul. Someone has to have me, no matter what the crazy world does. I can only show up if I am convinced I have a keeper of my heart and soul at all times. This must be an evergreen, eternal belief that I cannot alter in my power. It is the same for you. And He promises this to us, so you and I can both rest.

I mentioned this earlier that, at some point, mere survival and hanging on will not be enough. I've had seasons in my life when I was barely hanging on; this recent season has surely come close to that, and I know you've likely felt the same or still do. But in my experience hanging on eventually isn't possible anymore. The arms will give way. In the gym this is true of me with upper-body work (sooner rather than later) but even more in everyday life. So I can't afford to just hang on anymore.

Just hanging on leads to ignoring the soul because we operate in a mode of survival instead of growth, especially when it comes to our spiritual lives. And if we ignore our soul, we can't show up for our life as we want to.

We won't always be in a heavy growth period in our life. This is not about holding ourselves to a perfectionistic standard where it's always bells and whistles and God speaking to us from the configuration of our bagel seeds. (He's never done that with me, by the way.) But if we hang on for months and years without a plan to do more than that, eventually we will take ourselves out of the game of being used by God in the way He wants. A person who is merely hanging on can't be leading out in the kingdom of God—that's simply ineffective positioning.

Here's what I hope will be a helpful distinction, in case you feel like hanging on right now is the best you've got: holding on versus hanging on. You can do better than simply hanging on.

Holding on in the spiritual life is clinging to a stable place and being held in return. It is placing our lives on that big Hook that won't disappoint us (a very rough paraphrase of Romans 5:5). So, unlike simply hanging on, we aren't left to dangle in reliance on arms made of flesh. We are gripped by supernatural arms of immeasurable strength.

In hard moments each decision in these three areas of body, mind, and soul will mark you for well beyond that day. It is a showing-up versus shutting-down decision that determines who you become. The showing up may be harder at first, but in the end it will be the richest good—you will be the most well you have ever been. If you're someone who is tired of just being fine, this probably appeals to you. Personally, I'm done just being fine. It is the lowest level of living and doesn't cut it for me anymore.

In the beginning, showing up is often clumsy. So I don't want you to be discouraged if you're not good at it at first.

In hard moments you'll likely still be tempted to shut down your feelings, give people the silent treatment, revolt, and run away from pain. You'll want to brush your body aside when it's trying to tell you something or maybe even physically not show up at all. (Yes, sometimes we show up somewhere we don't want to, aka a family get-together with the in-laws we don't prefer, simply because it's one of those death-to-self moments I talked about that causes us to become a better person.)

You may be thinking, *What if I don't have a few minutes to react when I want to shut down?* Or *How can I do this when I am really, deeply hurt?* These are valid questions. Perfection isn't the goal. Sometimes you won't do this well. The point is to begin the practice so the next time you are presented with a show-up-or-shut-down option, you are better equipped. We don't become people most usable to God, maximizing our potential, overnight. We become them by practicing. And we are encouraged when we see in small, and often big, ways how we respond to things we know we would have responded to differently before: *I have truly changed here.*

The point of showing up is not just to say you accomplished something; it has everything to do with who you will become: a person God wants to use for the kingdom of God, even more powerfully than you can imagine. We are out there looking for all these ways to become wildly significant and viable. And yet *these* are the moments in which we are shaped. My cowboy-hat moment called for a thirty-second decision to engage in a needed character modification, years in the making. It started some neglected work in me that has continued still.

In case you aren't convinced that showing up when you want to shut down is the better way, please take a look at these comparative lists.

| shutting down leads to | showing up, on the other hand, |
|---|---|
| • broken relationships | • brings true joy over being the bigger/ better person |
| • resentment | • allows you to control your emotions instead of them controlling you |
| • isolation | • keeps you open and loving |
| • ingratitude | • ushers in an attitude of gratitude |
| • the inability to see the world positively | • gives you a new perspective about hard things |
| • bitterness | • eradicates resentment |
| • distance from God | • facilitates a deeper relationship of trust with the Lord |
| • the inability to produce great work | • brings on the flow of new ideas and dreams |
| • stunted emotional growth | • causes growth, change, and progress to occur |
| • unrealized potential/influence | • allows God to use your life |
| • apathy toward physical health | • creates a new care for your personal health |

I don't want to be like King Saul, who always gave himself a pass and never truly became God's man. I don't want to be a closed-off, bitter person, always suspicious and emotionally stunted. I don't want to have to keep shutting people out who want to love me. I don't want to keep feeling bad over actions I regret when my emotions bossed me. I don't want to squander away good gifts that God took care to create in me because I am unwilling to deal with my difficult feelings. I'm not willing to let my life be marked like that.

You're too precious for that, so I hope you feel that way too.

Don't forget: when it comes to our emotions, we always have a choice. On that note, I need to tell you one last thing about the John-lake story.

I knew I was showing up for my life that day on the lake when I snatched up my phone and started taking pictures of Mom and John.

We were about an hour into our boat ride when I happened to glance back and see Mom, holding her scarf around her neck like an older Jackie Kennedy, looking lovingly up at John. Beautiful, regal, honest, and kind, as always. But now the weariness of caretaking for so many years was gone. She looked almost young again. Her eyes danced with the excitement of new love but also with the wisdom of her years.

The object of her affection, cowboy-hat-wearing John, was tanned, with deep lines of experience from soul winning, rattle-snake hunting, and joke telling. He looked out over the crystal water with who-knew-what on his mind, then quietly reached out to hold her hand. No words were needed or exchanged as the boat hummed a love song.

And I, the voyeur, took it all in with clear eyes, seeing a story ordained by God instead of my own narrative clouded by pain. Quickly I fumbled for my iPhone and started covertly snapping pictures. I didn't want them to notice, to feel self-conscious and adjust a thing. I needed to remember how precious this was. I needed to feel it. I needed God to use that snapshot of His goodness to whisper to my heart, *I have you, Lisa. I always have, and I always will. Don't shut down even when it hurts. Show up for your life and watch Me heal your heart.*

He did, in so many ways, that very day.

It's been said, "The comeback is always better than the setback." I felt the truth of this in my bones out on the lake.

Friend, I don't know why your heart wants to shut down right now. Likely there is good reason. But I'm praying for progress. I'm praying this hard thing will become a precious good in your life. I am praying that, for all of us, our testimony becomes "Never before would I, but thanks be to God now I do."

We *can* become those showing-up kind of people.

☜

# CHAPTER 4

# doing what God wants even when it disappoints others

If you live for people's acceptance,
you'll die from their rejection.
—Lecrae[1]

YOUR ROAD TO GOD MAKING YOU INTO YOUR BEST AND MOST USA-
ble self will be littered with opportunities to cave to the pressure of
other people. These hard and uncomfortable moments, when you
refuse to disobey God and face disappointment from others in the
process, will shape you the most.

You could also call it *choosing to do the right thing*.

This is also where it can get confusing. *What is the right thing
to do?* we often ask. Just as with our current view of good (see the
intro for more on that), a lot of our confusion is often due to buying
into a skewed definition of what is right: The world's right thing
will be whatever feels right *to you*. It will require no other human's

governing or opinion. Because the denial of being a people-pleaser aligns with the spiritual call to deny people-pleasing, it can be easy to believe the entire message is in sync and then simply accept the rest of the world's life coaching about choosing the right thing for you. That is how Satan gets to us. He sneaks in a right message with a wrong one so we won't notice the wrong one so easily, or we become confused by it. Either way is fine with him because both work. I'm saying this loud and clear so we learn to recognize it: many times a wrong message won't be completely wrong. It will be almost right, with one-fourth of a deadly component. Please don't be so focused on the three-fourths of the message that you bypass the part that's the most lethal. Wherever he can, the devil will sneak it in to take you down by your eager acceptance of something that is partially right. He can, and he does.

I don't believe it's not that we don't know God's right thing for us most of the time. That should be good news if you have for years believed God may never give you more information about what's next. I believe it's that we either don't have the courage to do what we know is right (the signs are often pretty plain, everyday, normal things we ignore), or we have been reeled into the world's message of *whatever feels right to you is your right thing* by the correct part of denying other's opinions . . . and it hooked us into the other destructive part of choosing our preference over the will of God.

This is (again) how, while we don't change our anointing and appointing (or even our purpose), we are able to thwart our own usability.

If the world would add to its message of anti-people-pleasing *your right thing will be to do what God says, not what you feel*, then we could completely agree. But it won't do that because doing what God wants isn't an earthly agenda. Self is the god of culture.

Since the world won't do the right thing (see what I did there

☺), the real and only solution is for us to understand that choosing to do the right thing *is* to choose to do what God wants, not what other people or even we ourselves want . . . no matter what.

I've always wanted to do the right thing, though I haven't always done it. I've spent a lot of my life wishing God would just tell me what the right thing was. He often has, but listening to other people has caused that voice to get fuzzy and even muted, to where I have been talked out of it.

In 2010 I had just released a book called *{w}hole*, documenting much of my father's public fall from his pastoral position and my subsequent struggle to figure out who I was outside the definitions of strict religion, convoluted identity, and my difficult experiences with the church. Having crossed over from writing mainly for women to writing for men as well, I felt the weight of the expectation to produce accordingly, especially since a large publisher and another global organization that was a part of this project had taken a chance on me. No one needed to tell me I should do whatever was necessary for this project to succeed.

So I did. Every article they asked me to write to get my name out there, I wrote. Every interview they asked me to do, I did. Short notice for something? No problem. I jumped through impossible hoops to get it done and then some. *No* was not in my vocabulary. For months I nearly ran myself and my health into the ground. The season of book writing, rewriting (I wrote the book twice to "get it right"), and promotion left me in a state of physical and emotional exhaustion.

Perhaps the greatest irony of all in this is that somewhere along the way one of the things I had spent nearly a year and a half writing about—my delivery from a skewed identity—began to haunt me anew. This time it was a crueler identity crisis. It came down to how well I could perform, which most days left me feeling like a commodity more than a person. I wanted to succeed with watchful eyes on me, and the only way that was possible was for me to rise under the kind of pressure that is sure to make one sink. It wasn't enough for me to be me. I needed to be *more* me—more visible, more heard, more sought-after—in order to gain worth and career longevity. I quickly found out that when you're trying to be more, you often just wind up being empty.

This not only took a toll on my body. It messed with my head and heart and caused me to pull away from God. Where He had been calling me into a season of rest and a private, deeper relationship with Him, I was on a quest to get more visible. His plan was not working for me—it was inconvenient with the marketing and promotion other people were asking me to do. (Other people often get blamed for asking us to do too much, but we are the only ones who know where the asks are in conflict with God's leading. They can't possibly know that. Therefore, our schedule is ultimately our responsibility.) I felt sure He would understand and kept putting Him on the back burner. If I went with His plan, it would put me in direct opposition to publishing plans and potentially cost me my writing career, so I liked the publishing plan better.

> *When you're trying to be more, you often just wind up being empty.*

My *better* plan seemed fine until one day I found myself in a dire state, burned out and desperate to remember who I was outside of all the expectation, in a literal fetal position on the floor begging God for help. I was ready to quit writing, speaking, and anything else that involved doing much outside of daily survival. Finally being willing to shut out the noise of everyone else and get real with God is the only thing that kept me from quitting before I got to write the words of this book (and the others that have come in between). Actually, no. I *did* quit. I quit worrying about meeting anyone else's expectations and let God heal my heart.

I wish I always listened to God. No one has our best interests in mind more than He does.

The pull to please people is real. We all feel it. It starts when we are young and shadows us throughout life. Is it impossible to overcome? No—nothing is, with the help of God. But it's going to take attention, understanding, and effort, like all hard-good things.

To overcome it, we also have to face the hard truth that others' desires for us are often self-serving to some degree. Yes, even those we love and who love us. It's not that they are being purposely calculating. It is that all of us are skewed to want what most benefits us, and it's hard to be completely selfless in any situation. This makes listening to God for our next steps and choices all the more vital. As well-intentioned as any of us may be, the only One whose opinions and asks are without error or bias are the Lord's, so His should be the most trusted.

The scenario could look like anything—from saying no to the pressure of a friend or colleague to standing firm in a decision even a close family member might not understand or fully support. When we get used to hearing and responding to the Lord, we set ourselves up for a lifetime of obedience.

*When we get used to hearing and responding to the Lord, we set ourselves up for a lifetime of obedience.*

On the other hand, when we start feeding an early appetite for staying in the good graces of others, in lieu of doing as God prompts, we face a much longer process of breaking that pattern of approval seeking. Our parents may have taught us wisely to stand up for ourselves, not be lured into trouble, and not let others' approval of us determine how we feel about our worth (oh, frequently hurtful internet!), but even kids who aren't natural rule followers or people-pleasers still want to be accepted. Approval is a human, not a temperamental, need.

I first felt this pull at around the age of eight when my across-the-street playmate, Meghan, invited me over.

"Come upstairs," she said, wide-eyed. "I have something to show you." I followed behind her like a good soldier, not knowing what to expect. There, spread across the bathroom floor, were glossy magazines opened to reveal photos of men and women lying around in weird positions and body parts I'd never before seen.

"These are my dad's," Meghan whispered. "He keeps them under his bed."

My mind struggled to compute the porn I was seeing, and, at the same time, I could tell Meghan was excited to have an accomplice to this vile viewing party. But I heard a voice—a voice I'd been learning to recognize as God's—and it was unrelenting and specific. *Get up and walk out.* Despite my curiosity and eagerness to please my friend, I knew what God wanted me to do.

I was just a little girl who didn't know what it meant to have courage. I did not know exactly why seeing people exposed like this in a magazine was very wrong. But I knew what was the right thing, as we all do, deep down, when God tells us.

So I got up, ran down the stairs and out of the house, and never went back to Meghan's house again. If only I obeyed God that well every time, I wouldn't have plenty of other stories I regret.

I haven't always followed these three lessons, but they remain the most enduring and powerful ones of my life in choosing to do the right thing:

- Start listening to God early. Listen to Him to the end.
- Trust His voice the most. The flesh in the rest of us can't help but have motives.
- Do whatever it takes to follow Him.

## Persuasive Tactics

We will always have someone in our lives who has a strong opinion about what is best for us. These people are often not shy about offering their input, and many times they don't even try to hide their disapproval when we choose a different way. In those times we have to be willing to be disappointing. We also have to be willing to be misunderstood and possibly judged. These are hard pills to swallow, but I've been in all of these positions, and, I'm happy to report, you absolutely do not die from any of them. (You're still living, so the same is true for you.)

Here's where the hard and the good collide in our decision-making: Will we make a decision that feels better now or one that is better for us? It is hard to be misunderstood or have our plans or ideas rejected by people, but following God makes up for it in the long term. So if we can get past the temporary pull for approval, we are guaranteed to come out better.

For me, part of what helps to push past the momentary temptation to people-please is remaining aware of subtle persuasive tactics of the Enemy, which would get me off course. Here they are as a reminder:

### Compromise
*I'll just go halfway with God's ask to maintain relationships and keep peace.* This thought is often prevalent in situations where we are trying to remain neutral with a God-ask and we wind up bartering with Him to keep some measure of a comfort. God clearly told me to *get up and walk out of the house* that day at Meghan's, but my first instinct wasn't obedience; it was compromise. *Maybe I can just leave the room,* I remember thinking. Even young Lisa was trying to make deals with God.

But God's plan leaves no room for our counteroffers. The rich young ruler in Matthew 19 showed us that. He wanted eternal life, but he also wanted to keep his money. When the Lord asked him to give Him even that? Here was his response, in verse 22: "When the young man heard this, he went away sad, because he had great wealth."

*God's plan leaves no room for our counteroffers.*

When God asks us to do something a specific way, it is on purpose, not an oversight. Had the Lord wanted me to leave the house for my protection that day at Meghan's? Clearly, for reasons I can assume and ones I have no human access to. My mind and heart needed rescue. But maybe I needed saving in other ways, too, that I couldn't have even known. We don't know all that God does. Will we trust Him to know more than we do, or will we continue to believe what we see is the full picture? Proverbs 29:25 says, "Fearing people is a dangerous trap, but trusting the LORD means safety" (NLT). The only risk in life is to put faith anywhere else but in Him.

Bonus dad, John, likes to say, "Never make anything possible you aren't willing to have happen." It's one of his famous sayings, but it's ever wise. Ask anyone who has lingered somewhere a minute longer than their conscience told them to and an affair that happened as a result—they'll tell you they regret making their own heartbreak even possible. We save ourselves pain when we establish the ground rule that it's God who determines the rules for our life—not other humans and not us. You will never miss a minute of trouble you walked away from in obedience to God.

Let's talk about being a well-informed, open-minded person for a minute since I know we all like to be that. When we are making choices for our lives, gathering information by asking for wise counsel *is* important. But it is just that: gathering information. Our relationship with Jesus was always meant to be enough in its entirety to make wise decisions, which is why we all have individual access to the Bible and the Holy Spirit. That is not groupthink. When we're determined to stay open mentally to every possibility or idea without being rooted in the understanding we will eventually decide with the Lord, we can expect to continue to feel insecure. It can also lead to a harmful faith deconstruction—not the positive ditching-stale-spiritual-rigidity kind but the throwing-away-holiness kind that can wind up wrecking your life.

Compromise is one of those backdoor ways Satan uses in our relationships with other people to get us off track. Remember: it's the good-message-with-the harmful-message-lumped-together tactic. One of those messages is kindness to other people—such a righteous and biblical virtue but also the highest virtue, perhaps, of culture right now. But the world's kindness forsakes the motive rooted in godliness—a critical foundation. This void will eventually produce kind human beings who are kind in order to serve themselves. When you don't have the kingdom of God as your core, you eventually digress to a flesh motive.

In this, Satan is counting on us to want to be increasingly good humans. This is, again, in its purest form, a right quest. We should want to be good citizens, neighbors, upstanding people. But it's not the highest quest. Being like Jesus is our highest motive, which is on a different scale. It drives our behavior, which will result in, among other things, being a quality person. His plan always involves the transformative process that is for the good of us and other people and for His glory.

*Compromises don't produce nearly as much of what they promise.*

We don't have to look too far to see the crumb trail between what has dissatisfied us and what we have made possible by too much open-ended consideration. Compromises don't produce nearly as much of what they promise.

## Pressure

The pressure of our decision-making lives mostly in our mind.

Sure, people put pressure *on* us. But we can control what happens as we filter through the input they give. Though sometimes we flat out disobey God because we don't want to do what He says, most of the time we do it because we have a people problem. Ironically, our people problem isn't about other people. It is mostly about us.

The antithesis of the self-sacrificial call of the gospel is self-preservation. And self-preservation is in operation whenever we work to please other people rather than God, however that projects outwardly. Our culture doesn't make it easy on us. It pressures us to forget that our anthem as Christ followers isn't pleasure and indulgence but rather servanthood. Servanthood may at first sound synonymous with denying self to please others, but, remember, true people-pleasing is not about serving others. It's about serving ourselves, managing a perception of goodness in order to be accepted. Self causes us to turn away from doing what God asks in an effort to elevate human relationships—*for our benefit.*

*Ironically, our people problem isn't about other people. It is mostly about us.*

This is why too often we buy into the alternative of self-indulgence as the way to be set free from others' opinions (aka whatever feels right to you). But here's the wild irony: self-focus doesn't release us from desiring outside approval. *It fuels it.* We need more and more approval to continue to feel good about ourselves. So we are feeding the beast we mean to fight.

Doing what we know is good, not for our sakes but out of a desire to live passionately for the kingdom of God as healthy and whole people, is what sets us free from worrying about what anyone else thinks. At the same time, our Jesus-focus frees us to serve the needs of others and love them genuinely. Then in turn, we receive ultimate joy and pleasure. It is a cycle of constant nourishment to our own souls. But it starts with sacrifice versus indulgence, so the world can't fathom it. As believers, we have the foresight to know where our sacrifices are going, but the world doesn't. This is especially why we can't ask for outside approval from nonbelievers. People can't approve of a process they don't spiritually understand.

Being set free from the pursuit of man's approval was God's good idea, not our culture's. So don't let pretty memes take your eyes off Him. In Galatians 1:10, Paul wrote, "Obviously, I'm not trying to win the approval of people, but of God. If pleasing people were my goal, I would not be Christ's servant" (NLT). The only thing we leave out in modern inspiration is the God part. But that is the best part because while the world offers no real long-term solutions that break our people-pleasing habits, doing what God says takes care of that.

Besides the most important aspect of obedience, this is really the whole point of doing what God wants and asks: to take the guesswork out of your decision-making.

If you make decisions based on what other people want you to do, you will have successfully lived your life for other people. And you will live with the consequences of their choices for you.

If you make decisions based on whatever feels right to you without involving God in them, you will live life with a lot of complications. You will live with the consequences of your choices.

If, however, you choose to do what God says, you have a guaranteed template for problem-solving dilemmas: follow the Bible and the Holy Spirit, obey quickly, stay with the Lord, always. Rinse, repeat. And you will live with the assurance you are living whatever is the absolute best plan for you.

I know, even after all that, someone has this one lingering question: With all this talk about not doing what feels right to you, are you saying I shouldn't trust myself? Shouldn't I trust my God-given instincts?

Yes and no.

If by your God-given instincts you mean you have a feeling about something so you think that automatically means you should go with it because your gut is always right, I would just suggest you remember the times your gut has been wrong. I've yet to meet a person who was right one hundred out of one hundred times in their life about anything.

If by your God-given instincts you mean you are consistently praying and seeking the Lord, are reading the Word on a regular basis, possibly have even had some wise counsel on an issue, and have a settled sense of what you should do—though you have not had a sign appear in the clouds telling you which choice to make—I would say that is likely the Holy Spirit, and you aren't trusting yourself in this case. You are hearing from God.

## Selfish Desire

Doing what God wants will almost never be easy on the front end. If it's easy, if it doesn't stretch our faith in some way, it's likely our idea, not His.

Here's a deeper, tougher reality: our flesh may beg us to defy the voice of God. This is where it gets even more difficult. Lack of desire is one thing, but rebellion is another. Our flesh is every bit capable of rebellion. His asks may be inconvenient. Uncomfortable. Probably uphill. More than likely, they will require us to part ways with a desire of the flesh.

But this is where we must understand how hard and good go together. God did not design that His asks would just be hard without winding up good, even if, in the moment, we're not feeling that way. That is, again, why *doing hard things* only matters with a true godly promise, rather than merely being able to put that sticker on your laptop. This is also why the Christian journey can't be a feelings-driven journey. Our eyesight will lie to us and tell us what we see is beyond God's repair. Our heart will tell us it's too broken. Our lips will say exactly what they want, without holding back. What God wants is for us to be willing to go beyond the limits of our humanness. He will lead us there, but we must be willing to follow. So know that if it costs more than you are comfortable with, it's probably from Him. But also know that without Him life will be hard with no promise of it ever being made good. Call me a pragmatist, but I know which I prefer.

Before moving on, I need to make something clear. There will always be claims made "in the name of Jesus" that were not from Him. God, Jesus, and the Holy Spirit have been blamed for all manner of human nonsense. To excuse our poor decision-making ("God told me to . . ."). To add credibility to toxic relationships ("Jesus wants us to be together"). To validate us when we let our tongues run wild with harsh or foolish words ("I feel the Holy Spirit is telling me to speak up about this").

This might be the most important thing I say in this whole book: Do not use the almighty God as a scapegoat. Don't use Him for your purposes. Never manipulate someone in His name. Don't fear mishearing God. Fear misquoting Him. Fear it more than you fear being struck by lightning, getting a terminal illness, or going to prison. I say this not because I want to define Him dogmatically. I do so because I believe we ought to reverence His holy words that much—and for too long, we haven't. This is one of the disastrous results of doing what we want versus what God wants.

*Don't fear mishearing God. Fear misquoting Him.*

God's ask is a sure thing. Whether or not we see an immediate payoff, we can know His leading has absolute purpose.

Dietrich Bonhoeffer wrote, "God does not give us everything we want, but he does fulfil all his promises . . . leading us along the best and straightest paths to himself."[2] Yes, please. Give me more of God.

Have you recently been ignoring God's ask? Putting Him off? Trying to barter with Him to do it halfway and keep the peace in another relationship? Are you being nudged to set aside the approval and understanding of others to follow His unique call?

That thing He's asking of you is *for you*, my friend. And it may be about more than surface obedience. It may be for your very salvation. While our eternal salvation comes once and extends forever, God's grace continually rescues. God is in the habit of saving us from ourselves. He wants to save your heart, your mind, your time—your heart from the need of approval, your mind from going where it doesn't belong, and your time from being squandered on empty pursuits. He is so gracious to know exactly what surplus we have gathered in our lives that needs to go.

> *God is in the habit of saving us from ourselves.*

### ❧ GOOD: ❧
**Your obedience to God will bring rising confidence in future decision-making.**

---

*When we feel conflicted in the face of a dilemma, we're in good company.*

---

Jesus faced a dilemma when He had to choose between His ministry and His family's expectations (Matthew 12:46–50).

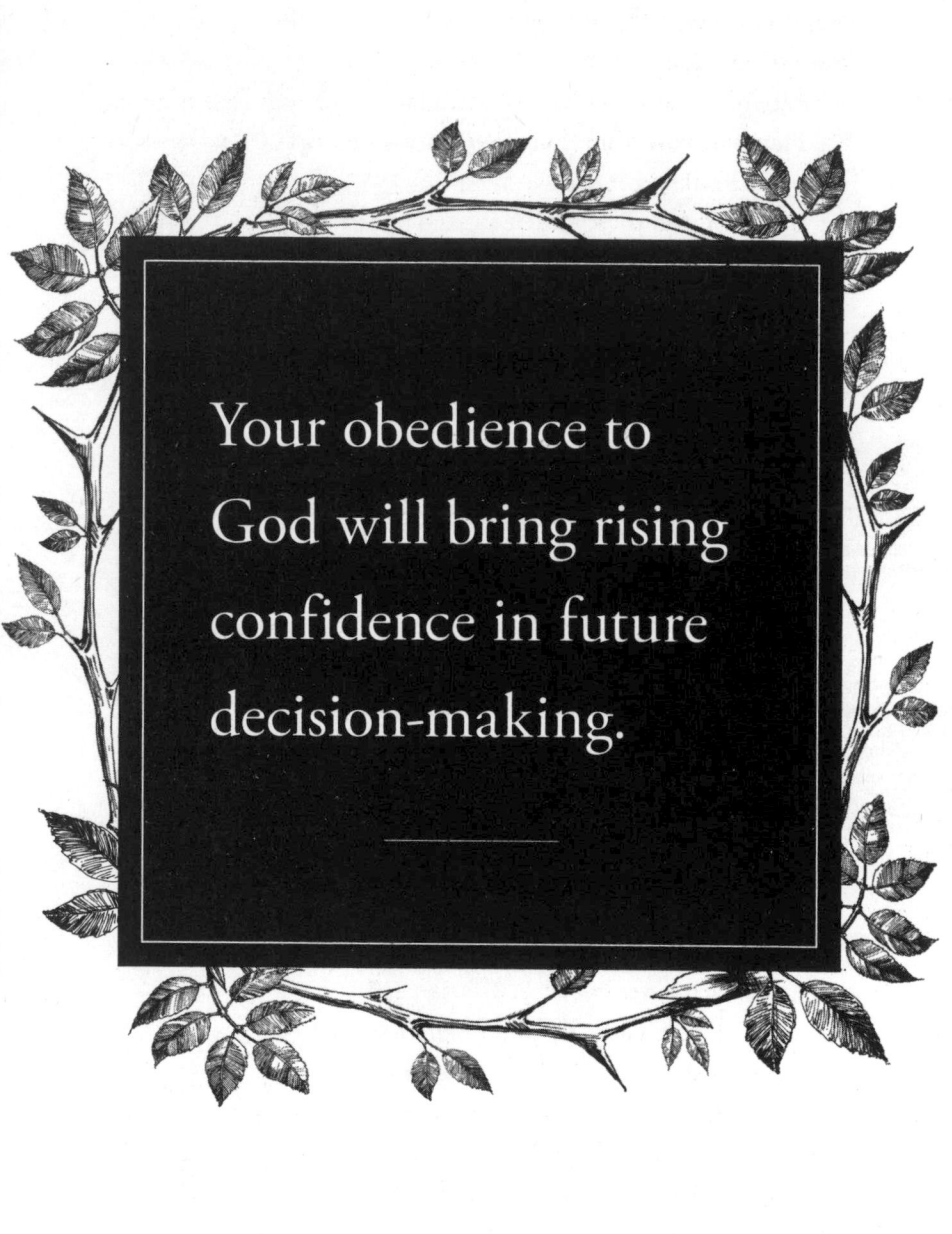

Your obedience to God will bring rising confidence in future decision-making.

Jesus faced another when He wanted to heal Lazarus, but His disciples opposed His return to the city where He had just been stoned (John 11).

A man whose father had just died faced a dilemma when Jesus told him to follow Him, but the man wanted to go and bury his father first (Luke 9:59–60).

Shadrach, Meshach, and Abednego faced a dilemma when they were told they must bow to an idol that went against their beliefs or be thrown into a fiery furnace (Daniel 3).

Daniel faced a dilemma when he was told he couldn't honor his conviction to pray only to God but instead had to pray to King Darius or be thrown into the lions' den (Daniel 6).

Mordecai faced a dilemma when he refused to bow to Haman and, thereby, risked death; and Esther, trying to save him, faced a dilemma of her own in the form of a deadly risk by approaching the king without knowing if he would accept her (Esther).

Jochebed faced a dilemma when she hid Moses, in disobedience to Pharaoh, to save his life (Exodus 1–2).

Hannah faced a dilemma taking her son Samuel to live with Eli, the priest, as soon as he was weaned rather than raising him in her home (1 Samuel 1).

So many of these examples remind us that doing what God wants often requires we die to what we love. Our relationships. Our reputation. Potentially, our very lives. This is hard, and—you already know—it's also good. If the risk is all we can see, we'll struggle to act. Our responsibility to God may not feel worth it. It may feel more like the worst possible idea. This is where faith comes in. The majority of our commitment to follow Jesus Christ happens in the aftermath of that first decision. Sure, it's hard to take that first step. But we don't follow Jesus

*Doing what God wants often requires we die to what we love.*

only for that moment when we first say yes. (That's the most life-changing and transformative, but it may not be as hard. Salvation? Heaven instead of hell? Life, not death? Someone we can trust guiding us? Yes to all that.) We follow Jesus for the moment and defect in year eight, but we remember that we once believed that His plan for us was the right one. That was the reason we chose to follow Him. It is not much of a commitment if it is only for the initial yes.

The yes has much more legs when it's still a good idea many years down the road; and with Jesus, it being the best idea forever is a *guarantee*. The frustration for a lot of believers comes not in the delivery part on God's end but on the expectation part on our end, where we will want equal input on the plan. We liked the initial decision to follow and the high moments, hence our conference-going and Bible-study binges. Who wouldn't?

But what if the richest part of the relationship is the part we attempt to block—uncomfortable moments with God when He shapes us for His greatest use of us? The hard good. God leading us with His supernatural eyesight down roads our human eyes weren't created to see because we likely see only the hard. We lose our own advantage by stopping God from leading us into higher, better places only He knows we are about to go. Our eyes see the five things around us and pick the best one and settle there, which will never be as good as God's design. This is why doing what God wants and asks of us is hard—but it is also so crazy good. The best outcome cannot be achieved by anyone but the Lord, *who can see it all*, and in order to get it, we do things His way.

As mentally weary as I am lately, just the thought of letting someone far wiser than me plan my life sounds like the best offer in the world. I can resist His plan, but why would I want to hinder something that will help me?

God's asks are scary for me too. Our attachments here make us worry that His plan may include an ask requiring too much. Follow Him and not get to bury a loved one? (Remember Luke 9?) Don't bow to the idol and get thrown into a fire as a result? (Daniel 3.) No, thank you. The extreme obedience in those biblical stories captures us for a reason. But surrender has no qualifier. These things I mentioned go beyond disappointing people to do what God wanted—some were literally matters of life and death. The truth is that more often for us it is death to self that is the hardest—the letting go of anything that might prevent us from caring more about it than obeying God.

In the case of Lazarus, Jesus' plan was the epitome of the hard good—He would, in fact, worry His disciples (Thomas even said, "Let's go, too—and die with Jesus" [John 11:16 NLT]), but He did it in order to bring life. The payoff was *resurrection*. It was worth temporarily disappointing in order to perform the miracle. If Jesus asks you to do something, it will have a more powerful point than you know.

So often in my own journey, crucial aspects of my life have hinged on one move, one divine connection with another person, one second interaction that only God Himself could have ordained. If someone in the equation hadn't listened to the voice of God to go to that particular store or place, our meeting never would have happened. You know what I mean because you've been there too. If we believe God knows, we have to believe He knows *all*: what is best for us, what is next for us, what is not for us, what is His will. We don't have to understand the intricacies of this to believe it is true and know that the path we want to follow is the one that has us doing what God says.

*If Jesus asks you to do something, it will have a more powerful point than you know.*

With the Holy Spirit whispering to our hearts and guiding us, we are faced with a spiritual dilemma. Will we ignore Him, or will we respond? Spiritual dilemmas are unlike moral dilemmas, in that we feel we have two moral duties, and we can honor only one of them, no matter our decision. When the Lord is asking something of us, there's no pro-and-con list to write down. But when we aren't fully sure if God is leading us into something, especially when our family or friends may not agree (or will be disappointed), as we seek God in prayer and also seek godly counsel, here are a couple of things to consider.

**IS IT SELF-SERVING?** Is the thing you believe God is leading you toward all about you or does it serve a greater kingdom purpose? Are you excited because it will add to your "good/powerful reputation" or because it will add to God's?

**DOES IT CONTRADICT SCRIPTURE?** Always check every potential assignment against the Word. The Bible stands the test of time as the source of all wisdom, and the clearest expression of God's character and His heart toward His children.

---

## Signs God Is Doing the Asking

"How do I know it's God telling me to do something?" This is a question I get a lot, for good reason. All of us want clarity on this. My friend Alli and I discussed it once, while we were both speakers on the docket at a Chicago women's event. Sitting in the greenroom together, between sips of hot tea, Alli turned to me. "Lisa, I think God told me to take my shoes off to preach. But I'm not sure if it was me or it was Him." She had that sort of look—the deer-in-the-headlights one that I had come to know myself when God dropped on me any sort of last-minute plans during a speaking assignment. Mumbling something about not having had a pedicure as she paced back and forth, all I could think of was not to get in the way of what God was clearly telling her to do. "What do you think?" she finally stopped and asked.

The words tumbled out of my mouth, blunt as I often am. "Would you tell yourself to speak without shoes on?" Wide eyes and silence between us, we let the question linger for a few seconds. Next thing I knew, she was peeling those shoes off like they were hot lava. *She knew. We both knew.* We all sort of know, don't we? Most of the time we ask these hypotheticals to buy ourselves time to do what we already know is right. It's not that we don't know if God wants us to do something. It's that we really don't want to do that something, so we double (and triple) check "just to make sure." If we question long enough, it could give us a potential out. I've done it this way plenty of times myself and talked myself out of following the voice of God.

So here are two tangible signs God is doing the asking:

1. He will ask you to do things you would never come up with yourself.

   I've found God to have a wild imagination, and He knows all the possibilities. As I pointed out earlier, His asks will often be out of the box, at times unconventional, and not in the least bit self-serving. But that doesn't mean you won't find deep satisfaction in the doing, despite the hard.

2. He will ask you to do things that are harder than you would require of yourself.

   It should be hard to do what God wants. He seems to prefer we depend on faith. If it's not hard, it might not be from Him. Does it feel right even though it's hard? God's asks always bring peace even though they are daunting.

Hard asks are where we have to land for a minute because this is where most of our struggle is rooted. We don't know how to tame our will to do what God wants. And yet, it is in understanding and prioritizing desire that we make some real progress. I believe in the principle of the greater desire, which is being willing to forgo what we want now for what we want most. This is a deal-breaking determinant of how we will live our lives.

This principle leads us to die to our desire to look at something our spirit tells us our eyes aren't meant to see (like me with Meghan and the magazines), something we really want to do in the moment if for no other reason than not to disappoint someone who wants us to do it with them (or ourselves, even—if you have developed a taste, sometimes the person you disappoint is *you*). Like, if God told us to shut our computers and walk away or run out of the house. In the end we get what we want more, which is to live with a clean heart and have a vibrant relationship with God and our spouses or whatever it is He has for us. If someone is encouraging you to stay unhealthy, never forget that people who aren't well don't like to be sick alone. So if you ever wonder why people aren't pleased with your newfound choice to get sober or stop doing something you used to do with them, there's probably a reason beyond them being sad they are losing their drinking buddy. (Real friends support a Holy Spirit–guided choice, no matter what.)

We also adhere to the principle of the greater desire when we forgo being understood by someone who is disappointed in our choice to speak up about an important issue in the church because God asked us to honor Him in this way. We trade it for what we want in the end, which is to be used to influence and encourage the body of Christ. We stand up for the gospel, which is the basis for both the bravery and passion for the cause.

I could go on with the examples. I don't know what it is for you, but I do know this: we will choose our priority, but only God's way will work. And I am convinced of this truth from C. S. Lewis:

"When we want to be something other than the thing God wants us to be we must be wanting what, in fact, will not make us happy."[3]

As you find yourself seeking the good in the hard practice of disappointing people to do what God wants, I'd love to offer a small help. As David often did as he wrote his psalms, speaking truth to your soul is a powerful spiritual practice. I've made a list of a few to start with. Type them in your notes on your phone or write them on a note card and put it on your mirror so you can see them when you're getting ready in the morning.

- Others don't have to understand or approve of me.
- God hasn't called me to the ministry of *over*explaining myself. Or *over*apologizing. Or *over*analyzing.
- God is for me. He desires for me to have joy.
- God will never ask me to do anything that will bring me harm.
- Going against others' expectations may be hard, but God's plan will ultimately be good.

## On the Other Side of Needing Approval

A deep, white blanket of snow wrapped a gorgeous corner of Pennsylvania. I was there more than five years ago, preaching a weekend retreat messages from Revelation 2 about wanting God most. We'd already covered some solid ground, and God had done some good work. As a speaker, I've been to a lot of places. This is one that has never left my mind.

It was the last message, at the point when I ask the women to respond to God in this tangible way: write on white note cards what God has told them during the weekend that they need to surrender to Him.

"What do you want God more than?" I ask them, and I take it one step further. I tell them that I do not want their "top of the pocket" response—meaning that quick, churchy response a lot of us have grown accustomed through the years to give at a time like this. "I want the bottom of the pocket response," and they know exactly what I mean. That harder admission, the one that is buried a bit lower, that may take a more painful unearthing.

I requested one final action—to bring their written white note cards to the front and lay them on the altar, which was really just basic auditorium stairs. I love the idea that no fancy attempts were made at this event to dress up the place the women were to lay their cards. I was at the place in my ministry that I longed for all of us just to be ourselves and find extravagances difficult. I asked the musician to play, as usual. I prayed, and one by one the women began to come down front. It didn't take long for the front of the room to be alive with scattered white papers, anonymous with words that represented lives and situations known only by God, laid wherever the women had put them, perfect in their spots. A few minutes passed, and the room was hushed with now seated women, deep in prayer and thought over what they'd just laid bare before God.

But there was one more woman.

To this day I do not know her name.

She brought her card to the front but did not lay it down. Instead, she stood in the middle of the room, holding it like it was the last thing she had on this earth, and she sobbed in a way only people who know what giving up the thing they love the most looks like. I can still see her now, black jacket, hands clenched tightly in the front, shoulders shaking, an unquieted wail between gulps. I was the speaker in the front, who just minutes before was about to wrap things up, and then, suddenly, something inside me broke too, and I fell to my knees and sobbed with her.

I know what it is like not to want to listen to God when He talks. And I know what it's like to know I will, no matter what, do the very best thing and say yes even though in the moment it breaks my heart.

Sometimes God will ask us to run out of a house when someone wants us to stay, and it will disappoint them.

Sometimes He will ask us to speak up, and people will have preferred we stayed quiet. He'll want us to adopt a child or sell our home or change careers, but our people won't all understand. He'll want us to make a move that others don't support.

And it won't always be selfish of the people to be disappointed. Sometimes they will just love us so much they will want what they believe is for our best. But when we get to the point where we are willing to disappoint people to do what God wants, we will have become the most usable version of our created selves. Because that is when we will always obey God, no matter what.

When I think about that woman at the altar clutching her card, I think of how that moment marked me forever. But I also think about what came next—the thing that I never got to see when she went home. I think about the peace and strength. I think about the joy and release of whatever she had been holding. You don't sob like that and not get a payoff from giving something big over to God. The truth is it should be that hard to lay down our wants. We should take it that seriously. We should each be the last one at the altar because we can't stop wanting more of God there.

It's hard to disappoint people, yes, but the other side of that is the exhale, the assurance, and the spiritual growth. These are the things that make us never look back when we disappoint people all over again.

CHAPTER 5

# finding joy in the waiting

Now is no time to think of what you do not have.
Think of what you can do with what there is.
—Ernest Hemingway, *The Old Man and the Sea*[1]

Somewhere along the way in my adult years, I picked up an unhelpful practice: the more I learned of the immense pain others carried through this world, the more I minimized my own everyday struggles.

When the kids were little, and many days didn't feel precious, I was especially hard on myself. *Suck it up, Lisa. A lot of women would love to have kids, and you're whining just because you haven't slept in a few days?* I lectured myself. *You're fine.*

Sleep-deprived mothering wasn't the only time this showed up. It cropped up again when my father was sick and dying, and I noticed myself hesitating to share the depth of my sorrow, knowing some friends had lost their fathers much earlier. After all, I'd had mine for more than forty years. I felt selfish, as if someone who had mourned their loved one longer ranked higher up on the hard scale. (Never mind that sleep is important, mothering is hard enough already, and loss is loss, no matter the length of time.)

*The struggle Olympics.* Perhaps you, too, have competed in them: I had to have a hysterectomy, but that person got cancer. My husband had an affair, but hers got the woman pregnant.

Other times the tables are turned, and we're the ones minimizing someone else's pain, convinced our hard thing is worse than they could know. Even though *we don't actually know.*

Rating pain. We often do this. And it leaves us feeling very alone, resentful, and isolated. Author Brené Brown offers this insight:

> The exhausted doctor in the ER in New York does not benefit more if you conserve your kindness only for her and withhold it from yourself or from your coworker who lost their job. The surest way to ensure that you have a reserve of compassion and empathy for others is to attend to your own feelings.[2]

I like this responsible way of thinking.

Hard is hard. Pain is pain. We need to stop comparing them.

It's a lesson to be learned before we wrestle with the uncomfortable inevitability of having to wait on God, which—in the scheme of a world with its much more pressing issues that feel like a burning-down house in recent years—doesn't garner a lot of empathy. But it is hard to wait on God. We've all been there and know it. It is actually one of those things that can create real resentment . . . an eventual breach between us and God. Especially if we minimize how the pain is affecting us—while allowing its reality to damage our hearts.

## Impatience Leads to Mistakes

My mother got married at the wee age of twenty, so by the time I was twenty-two, I dramatically deduced I must be doomed to always having a mattress with a one-sided indent. Since childhood I had dreamed of being a wife and mother. But when I got to the age it could become possible, God wasn't moving as quickly as I'd hoped. I sat in seminary—full of lots of find-your-future-spouse-here talk—single, thinking all manner of assumptive, gloomy thoughts. What if twenty-two turned into sixty-two and my dream never came true? It was silly, but emotional baggage can make you think that way. The year before, my life had taken a drastic turn. After a hard breakup with a fiancé, I'd been left with a monogrammed cake cutter and a dress. Now I was starting over in grad school in a different state where I knew no one, and time appeared to be ticking away. I was *practically turning ancient.*

Struggling with my self-esteem, I was sure it was impossible to get proposed to twice, since it turned out that the one man who did ask me to marry him didn't really want me. As my impatience with God grew, I began to take things into my own hands.

The problem with impatience is that it leads to mistakes. I learned this very quickly. Here are three things I personally experienced being impatient and where that can lead us:

### 1. Compromise what we truly want

In my desire to find a husband, I went on many dates in seminary—more than I care to remember or discuss here. Some should never have happened. On one date a guy I was already pretty sure wasn't *the one* when I said yes to go out sealed it when our dinner plans—after he got us lost, drove us around for four hours, and refused to stop for directions—ended up with us eating steak at 11:30 p.m. Another guy picked me up in a car with a burned-out back seat and ash floating around my head. (Why was it burned out? I still do not know.) It wasn't just bad dates. I manipulated some men too. I regret the time I flirted with a guy who had a long-running crush on me, someone I never would have considered, getting his hopes up, just so I would have a date.

Thank goodness none of these were bad guys. I know it could've been far worse. I've had some of those experiences, too, with much harder memories. But in each case that I compromised, I talked myself into a date and hurt myself or someone else in the process. I knew what I was looking for, but I didn't want to wait around to find it.

Impatience added to limited vision makes anything seem reasonable. We don't want to think of rushing as a lack of confidence or even a lack of belief in God, but we have to consider it. Taking matters into our own hands is a sign of distrust. Otherwise, we would find rushing unnecessary. David said in Psalm 5:3, "In the morning I lay my requests before you and *wait expectantly.*" If we struggle with rushing God, it's good to look at our expectations: Do we expect God to disappoint us? Or do we expect Him to come through?

> *Impatience added to limited vision makes anything seem reasonable.*

I know we're tempted to give the churchy answer, but let's give the honest one instead. This is not a matter of name-and-claim theology—it is a matter of truth. God can be trusted. God knows more than we do. Therefore, waiting instead of compromising changes nothing about His plan. Most of the time our hurried decisions are historical: we let our past convince us God *won't* because He *hasn't yet.*

But we don't know what all He does.

## 2. Retreat to what we know

An ex-boyfriend, one I loved deeply, reentered my life while I was in seminary. Wanting so much to find the man I would spend my life with, I reverted to what I was familiar with even though I knew it was wrong. It was thrilling to have another go at our relationship. He showered me with attention and said all the right things about how this time it would be different. My heart wanted so desperately to believe it was true and experience love being rekindled that I couldn't recall any of the old reasons we broke up. Never mind that he hadn't been good for me back then and our compatibility level had not changed. The only difference was I'd grown tired of waiting on God.

Often, when we get impatient, we cash in our good sense. It's not that our circumstances change; it's that our willingness to stay wise for a prolonged period of time might. We view familiarity out of rose-colored glasses. We long for the comfort of what we knew because at least we had *something*. What was once not what we wanted, for good reason, has been accepted in an impatience haze. David, again, wrote us a beautiful patience anthem for moments like these. Psalm 40:1 says, "I waited patiently for the LORD; he inclined to me and heard my cry" (ESV). It is easy to go back to what we know. But it is better for us when we wait on God instead.

## 3. Take matters into our own hands

In any waiting scenario, as I wait on God to do what I want, I often become more and more frustrated. During my season of disappointment, gloomy thoughts, and desire to rush God's plans for my life in seminary, the one and only thing I was sure of was that He wasn't doing what I wanted. Like all situations where we cannot see past our own desires, I was convinced He wasn't listening to me. And when we think God isn't listening to us, things can get especially rocky.

I began daydreaming about how I could make something happen with someone—often, scenarios that didn't even make sense. I considered calling old boyfriends in case I had somehow not recognized that they had been the one. I thought of transferring to a different school in the event my husband was over there somewhere. (*Maybe I had gone to the wrong school!*) Outlandish considerations became my pastime. After all, God sure wasn't helping dream things up. When you lose

*When you lose faith in God, you do lots of plotting.*

faith in God, you do lots of plotting. If He is no longer trustworthy to manage your life, it becomes a wild scramble to make up for His lack.

Nearly every mistake I've ever made in any scenario in which I didn't want to wait on God has been marked by these behaviors: compromising, reverting, and taking matters into my own hands. Maybe you relate? I've tried it when I've wanted something to happen with my career and God was taking too long to deliver. When I've wanted something to happen with our housing. When I've wanted to hurry along relationship potential. Without fail, my desire to push God faster has resulted in messy complications, and I've visited heartache upon my own soul.

When God makes us wait, it's because He wants to save us from something, give us something better, or form in us something we need. For me to write this, it rolls right off my fingertips. For you to highlight it probably feels right too. But living it is a whole different, hard story.

But it is good, and we can judge by the fruit it yields. When we have to wait on God, we have to need God. We have to open

*When God makes us wait, it's because He wants to save us from something, give us something better, or form in us something we need.*

up our hearts and express our deepest desires to Him. Sometimes we have to linger long enough to get something out of our system that was a bad idea.

And we are forced to find the new thing that is the actual right thing. Get that? All those things I mentioned are for *us*. They are for developing deeper communication with the Lord, helping us make fewer mistakes, and giving us greater opportunity to discern and do the right thing. Meanwhile, we develop character we'll never regret in places we otherwise wouldn't. Developing character sometimes doesn't feel worth it until years down the road. I wish we could get all the good things right away and become better people automatically. But waiting is one of the best producers of good things.

## What We Think We Need

There are many things we absolutely need in life—food, a place to lay our heads at night, and a way to provide financially to pay for them. Much else is likely debatable, but we're human, so the list of what we *think* we need is much, much longer. When we don't get these things that are more wants than needs, we can begin to feel as though God is purposely withholding good things from us.

I've arrived at five expectations that often drive what we think we need—thus, our frustration with God while we wait. This is different from waiting expectantly on God as David suggested. Our human expectations are opposed to a godly expectation that He will work on our behalf on His terms. Our needs are often shaped by these things:

1. our ideas
2. our assumptions
3. our view of the potential in something
4. our fears
5. our tendency toward comparison

Soak that in for a minute. Any of these play into your own frustrations? Remember, we have finite understanding. Our ideas, for instance, might be great. But we can't really have *all* the information needed to know if they'll work. Our assumptions work this way too.

I'm living this in real time right now, as we've been scouring the internet looking for a house to buy. Partly because of COVID and partly because I'm an introvert who doesn't like leaving the house, the convenience of this is the only part of looking for real estate I have enjoyed since we moved to a rental home and abandoned our plans to build. It's easy for me to get excited and start having incredible ideas for a place I've never even seen in person. I can assume many things about the home and property as well. Just the other day I fell in love with a gorgeous white-brick ranch house. Based on the photos alone, I was ready to make an offer that very day. I couldn't fathom what could possibly be a snag. I had done all the internet research, including Google Earth, studied every image, sleuthed every public record from the county. This house was perfect.

But when we finally went to look at it, we discovered there was a neighborhood going in next door that couldn't be seen in any of the photos. While the internet listing made the house look incredibly secluded, new homes were being built extremely close to the house we wanted to buy. Inside, parts of the floors were buckling. And there were other unforeseen issues. All of my assumptions about this house and ideas for buying it and making it our dream home were awesome, but if I'd been given more information, I never would have gotten so excited about it. It was far from the perfection I was initially sure it was.

Only God has the supernatural vision to see past our earthly ideas and assumptions.

The potential we see in something often colors our belief it will automatically play out the way we think it will. That can then lead us to a skewed train of thought: If God is withholding from us, it couldn't be because we're wrong about how things might turn out. Surely we couldn't be mistaken about the potential we imagine or see. This excruciating wait must be because He doesn't want us to be happy.

> *Only God has the supernatural vision to see past our earthly ideas and assumptions.*

Except that's not how God works.

Though our happiness is not His ultimate goal for believers (hint: it's holiness, sanctification; see Romans 6:18, 12:1, and 1 Thessalonians 4:3), He is a good Father who still wants us to have wonderful things. They just might not be the *same* things we want, at least at the moment. This is where belief is tested: when we trust His plans when ours don't match. We would settle. He *won't*. It is the wise, loving parental nature (also supernatural) that allows Him to be able to watch us be uncomfortable in a process He knows is for our good. This is not cruelty; it is ultimate love. He is even willing to be the object of our anger in order to accomplish His best work in our lives. It's normal in the midst of a hard waiting period to struggle with this. But if we continue to struggle with believing this to the point our hearts are becoming hardened, it may be time to ask ourselves: Deep down, what do we really believe about the character and heart of God?

We do see things wrong all the time. We make bad choices because of our fleeting desires and inaccurate assessments. The implications for these tendencies are clear in the Word. Romans 13:14 says, "Put on the Lord Jesus Christ, and make no provision for the flesh to gratify its desires" (CSB). (He knows we want what we want.) And Proverbs 3:5 says, "Trust in the LORD with all your heart and lean not on your own understanding." (He knows we think we know best.) Undoubtedly the Lord knew how much our vision would be clouded beyond our ability to see past a fogged view. He knew we would fully believe in what we understand things to be. That is why we aren't good at seeing another person's opposing viewpoint—to us, it is perfectly clear why our perspective is the right one and they are dead wrong. Enter complicated relationship dynamics. Hello, every election season.

But that's not all.

As we choose our assessments in lieu of God's plan, we dive deeper into our egos. This causes myriad problems, due to our massive investment in the need to be right. Even in an election, for example—if we really got down to the core—we have to consider how much of our anger and disillusionment, if we wind up on the losing side, is due to our human need to win, not the virtuous rhetoric we claim. We may want those things we fight for in the voting booth, but if we strip all that away, it's not unlike that game of Yahtzee we simply hate to walk away from having just lost. I'm not watering down the crucial issues of our time to a silly game—I live in the real world too. But our behavior sometimes sure seems as if we think we are playing chess.

Waiting on God is no different. We want to win whatever prize we are hoping for. We are impatient because waiting feels like losing. Someone else wins while we lose; we miss out while others get ahead; we are told no while someone else hears yes. Our desire for immediate gratification grates against God asking us to say yes to the reality of never being gratified in the way we think is best. That is not easy.

But as we are willing to do things God's way, we also do not live in the angst of needing to be satisfied on our terms. That is good, both in the long term and short, because life with this kind of gamble is anxiety producing. As I mentioned before, secular philosophy tells us to trust ourselves and just do what we want, but that is monumentally risky. That approach doesn't *truly* care about our long-term mental health. It's just out to sell us on something it knows we want to hear right now. Trusting ourselves has proven to be the worst possible thing at so many points in our lives. Otherwise, we'd all have a track record of perfect choices. We wouldn't have to regret the late-night tweet or other larger actions we can't take back. This is why having Jesus in our lives is a lifesaving strategy—not just eternal but for daily living as well.

Back when I was re-dating my ex-boyfriend, my father sat me down for a blunt one-on-one to snap me back to the reality he could easily see, which, in my clouded judgment and desires, I could not. "Don't get caught up in the person you hope he will become," he said. "Make a decision based on the person right in front of you." I was forced to admit that while this guy might well grow into the best husband and father one day, the signs of how he would treat a woman in the long run were looking quite grim based on the way he was handling me in the present. This was the best relationship advice I ever got, and after some months of stubborn refusal to see the truth, I finally took it to heart. We broke up, which no doubt saved us both from a lifetime of incompatibility and heartache.

Chasing after people and things because we see potential, rather than seeing them as they actually are, is not generally a wise way to live. I understand you might read that and think I'm advocating for not giving people a chance, but that is not true at all. I'm always for the underdog, to the degree that, in a room of both extremes, I struggle to be attracted to the side that is popular and successful. The problem is in the emphasis. It is not about honoring the potential in people by believing the best in them. It is about counting on the things we see to change because symptoms suggest the possibility exists. We can give people the courtesy of hope and belief without entangling our lives with theirs too deeply. This is another one of those two truths that can coexist: people can have potential, but we can also make the best decision for ourselves based on who they are right now in our lives.

Fear can also drive what we think we want. Fear of being alone our whole life. Fear of being misunderstood. Fear of not being chosen. Fear of not getting to experience being a mom. Fear of not being seen as capable if we don't get that job. I diminish none of these. They are real. What about the pressing fear of not having provision? Never before has this fear felt so close. A girl who got married before she turned twenty-five and has enjoyed her dream of motherhood isn't exactly one to preach to anyone on the ache attached to the longing for a family. I'm in no way demonizing any of these needs and desires. I recognize the gap between my youthful frustrations and the reality I know now with life experience under my belt. But that's just it. The wanting and waiting is always urgent to us in our situation. We are convinced of what we see and believe. And God cares about how that affects us, regardless of how accurate the view is or how much others verify it.

What I'm asking of you is to not let fear make your decisions. When we make a habit of letting fear decide, we find ourselves owned by a cruel and unrelenting master. We make rash decisions out of a panicked mindset. Our frenzy causes a further breach between us and God, which then deepens our fears. This is the vicious cycle of want and need based in fear.

And finally, of course, playing the comparison game drives frustration in our lack. They have a three-thousand-square-foot

*What I'm asking of you is to not let fear make your decisions. When we make a habit of letting fear decide, we will find ourselves owned by a cruel and unrelenting master.*

house with a pool, so where is ours, God? They have that dream job, but we've worked just as hard. They posted vacation photos of smiling kids in floaties, swimming at the beach. We haven't had the money to go anywhere in ten years. Doesn't God also care about our need for rest and relaxation? In our deferment, we feel behind. Before we know it, we're way down that mental rabbit hole, hearing those deceptive whispers. *God doesn't love you enough to give you the good gifts.* Then comes the resentment, the dissatisfaction, and the potential shutting out of God. Recognize the cycle?

This is where the hard lives. It is where the risk of being disappointed lies, but also the benefit of peace, if we turn to God instead of ourselves. So here we are, again, living in the tension. I suppose this is why the Lord so often says in the Bible, *I'm right here—call anytime! You're going to need me!* (Lisa's very loose paraphrase of Jeremiah 33:3, among multiple others).

In the past maybe you haven't been able to make peace with waiting on something because that human tendency to grab life by the collar and take action has made it unnecessary to do so. Every time God has begun to help you make progress, you've reverted to autonomy again. So many times we go to the weeds because we tire in the waiting. Weed living represents where we reside during our desperate days. I know it well myself. We normally wouldn't dare live in the weeds, where we settle for a lower level of living versus God's abundance, but God is taking too long. So in our boredom, and out of the sheer pull to make something happen for ourselves, this is where we walk.

So what's the solution? If waiting is hard and it is a part of life, how do we live so we stay out of the weeds? How do we walk the hard-good path?

Excellent questions.

I'll meet your questions with a few of my own. What *do* you have right now? In what way can you keep so busy serving Jesus that you don't have time to miss that thing you're waiting on? On the days I feel the most frustrated with God for not working out the plan I want, I often think of the incredible Joni Eareckson Tada, one of my longtime heroes of the faith. In a wheelchair since her diving accident as a teenager, she made much of her paralysis. Her art through writing, painting, and music has had an impact on millions of people, including me. What if she had waited to engage with life until she had proof of whether she would ever walk again? What if she had waited for the Lord to heal her body to use her gifts for the kingdom of God? I'm so grateful she did not. In the words of Ernest Hemingway, "Now is no time to think of what you do not have. Think of what you can do with what there is."[3]

Let's do *that*.

## ᔥ GOOD: ᔢ
### Your perspective will shift from *desert darkness* to *pause with purpose*.

*You'd be hard-pressed to find any better example, biblical or not, of someone who did his time waiting than David.*

A testament to faithful waiting, David is one of our go-tos for how-to and for good reason. Not only did he wait—he waited well. To me, that's harder. I can wait if I absolutely have to, but I can't guarantee I'll be in a good mood. Waiting without waiting well is difficult. There's nothing remarkable about going through something you had no say in. There's also nothing special about waiting and becoming bitter or mad. A lot of us do that.

What takes this up several notches and sets someone like David apart is that whenever he was stuck living in the in-between, *he wrote songs.* From the time he was promised he would be king to when he was finally enthroned. All throughout a long, risky season of being pursued by his enemies until he no longer had to live on the run. You can read in 1 Samuel 16 where God promised David a position he wouldn't deliver on for fifteen years. I know what kind of mental state I would be in if I had to wait that long for God to make good on something He'd promised me—not great. But David passed his time writing lyrics of praise—and often angst. This is remarkable. To do that, you've got to have the real stuff.

As a creative myself, I know that a hitch in my day can alter my ability to piece together even one sentence, let alone paint an entire brilliant, poetic narrative like any one of David's psalms. David never faked being fine. He lived in constant tension and with a desperate desire to get from A to B. Yet despite enduring long uphill battles and waiting on promises that seemed they'd never come to pass, he remained in a good place with God. Generational healing to our souls has come through his words because of it. (I personally read a psalm almost every day.)

In trusting God in your waiting, do not dismiss the idea that someone is being inspired to follow suit. This is where your desert darkness becomes a pause on purpose—your hard being used by God for the good of someone else.

So I ask you this question: Would you wait differently if you knew God would use it for His glory?

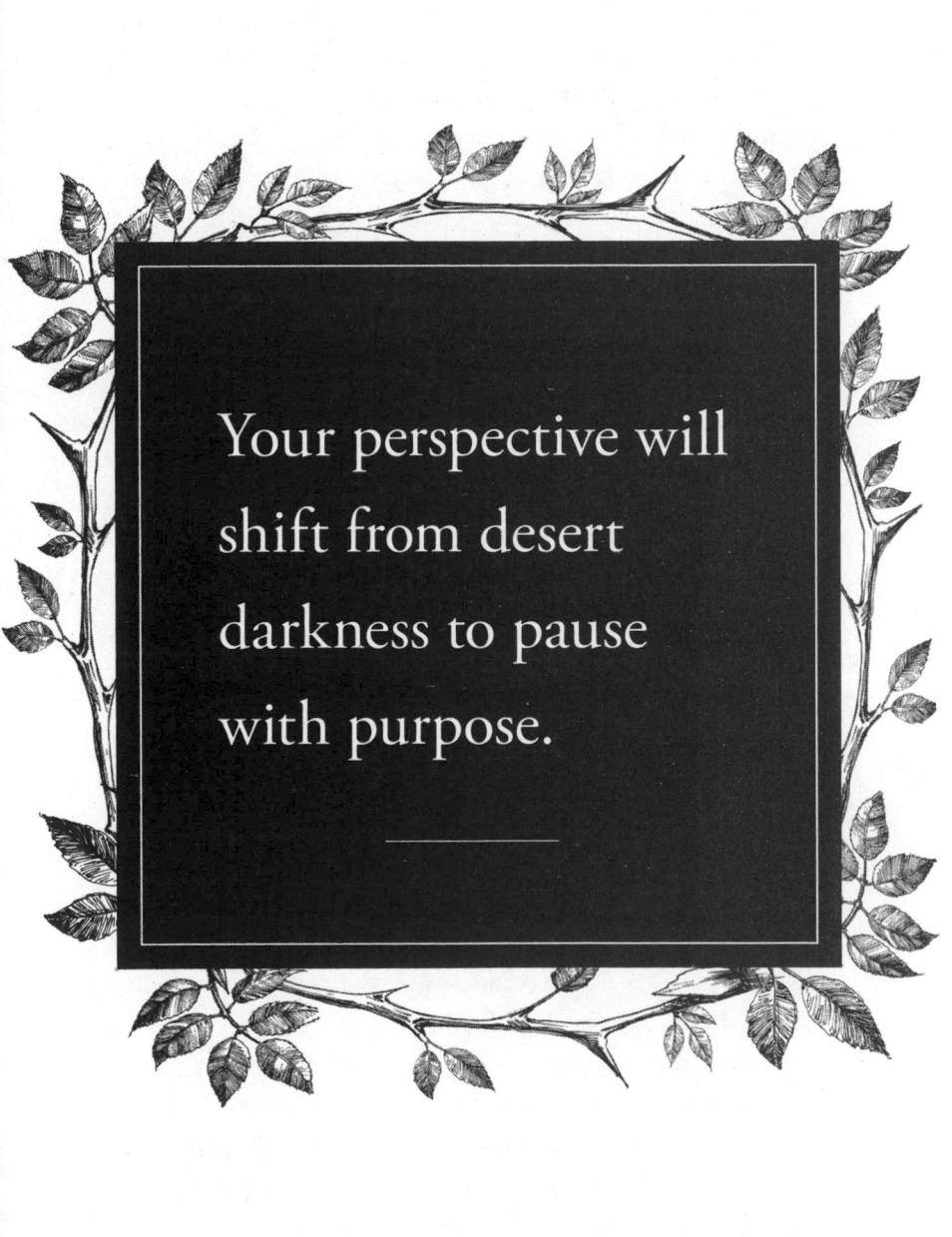

Your perspective will shift from desert darkness to pause with purpose.

John 5 talks about a man who "had been an invalid for thirty-eight years," waiting by the pool of Bethesda for healing (v. 5). This story—one I have written and taught about multiple times—continues to mark my life because of the way God changed everything in what had been a historically long and unchanging situation. The reasons for the man's excruciatingly long wait are unclear, but what we know for sure is Jesus had the touch that healed the man's life. I've lived longer than his almost forty-year wait period, so I can only imagine how long that would feel. It would be more than difficult for me to wake up positive every morning, much less muster up true faith.

But please think about this. The minute God healed that man, I can only guess that he wasn't thinking about being sidelined for thirty-eight years with a sense of resentment. He had only a sense of sheer joy. In that moment of healing, it was worth all the years of waiting to be well.

> Question: Would you wait differently if
> you knew healing was coming?

Simeon waited well. He deserved props for his years of prophesying the Messiah would come, but he didn't want credit. He just wanted to see the Messiah.

Now there was a man in Jerusalem, whose name was Simeon, and this man was righteous and devout, waiting for the consolation of Israel, and the Holy Spirit was upon him. And it had been revealed to him by the Holy Spirit that he would not see death before he had seen the Lord's Christ. And he came in the Spirit into the temple, and when the parents brought in the child Jesus, to do for him according to the custom of the Law, he took him up in his arms and blessed God and said,

"Lord, now you are letting your servant depart in peace,
    according to your word;
for my eyes have seen your salvation
    that you have prepared in the presence of all peoples,
a light for revelation to the Gentiles,
    and for glory to your people Israel."

(LUKE 2:25–32 ESV)

I imagine Simeon's steadfast insistence on a coming Messiah was not always met with warmth or enthusiasm. Waiting for it to be proven true had to have been hard. A history of trust in his God gave the ability for this. The anticipation of seeing the One he loved made the wait worth it.

Question: Would you wait differently if you knew you would more clearly see and know Jesus through it all?

Waiting isn't just for you. It is often for God to do a great work in and through you—showcasing a relatable struggle so someone else can see how His presence in life is a game changer. Think of testimonials you've heard through the years. Stories have the power to alter the way we have hope. It is why you often hear it said: your story matters. It's not just stories with details of being rescued from a wild life that God restores that touch our souls. It's also stories of radical endurance to the faith. Would you wait differently if you knew your story of faithfulness was going to shine a bright light on Jesus for years to come and inspire others the way David's, the lame man's, and Simeon's stories inspire us?

Some of us have been praying for a very long time to get out of a stale or nearly dead spiritual life, and we've run out of great ideas. We have wanted for years to see change in ourselves. We've been begging for God to use our lives, year after year. What if

121

the uncomfortable process of waiting on God helped us with this movement? What if we could finally become the person we've been praying to be for years? What if God wants to use us through our testimony of waiting, but we keep rejecting it?

God often transforms us with things that are right under our nose.

---

                         ଞ

## What You See Isn't What You Get

When you visualize Peter stepping out of a boat and attempting to walk across a lake to meet Jesus, what do you see?

I see Jesus intentionally surprising His disciples in the middle of the night, allowing them to experience fear and awe so they would know He was indeed God. And I see a picture of what happens when we measure how we're doing by our immediate physical circumstances.

In Peter, I see you and me. In Matthew 14, he first had his eyes locked on Jesus, and he was doing well. But then he turned away his gaze. He looked away and started to sink. That's us, when all we can see is our suffocating financial situation and the fact that God has not yet delivered us from it. That's us, when we hear laughter coming from a minivan full of kids, and disappointment steers our emotions off course because another month went by without a positive pregnancy test. That's us, when we see a ministry we feel ready for but no opportunities seem to come our way. That's us, when the world looks really bad, and we crumble in fear.

Our eyes and ears tell us things aren't good. They tell us to worry. They tell us to take matters into our own hands, that God isn't going to come through for us as we want, that our future is every bit as bad as we believe, based solely on what we can see in front of us.

Even when the symptoms seem clear and the elements are especially unrelenting, don't go on what you see. That is the unique distinctive of following the Lord. We don't use our eyes; we go on what we know to be true about God. If disappointment can be historical, so can faith. The call to remembrance is perfect for these times, when the waves of life are especially threatening. It's nothing new—the church at Ephesus (and every other one) struggled to remember God and in the process lost their way. "You have forsaken the love you had at first. Consider how far you have fallen! Repent and do the things you did at first" (Revelation 2:4–5).

It is for our good not to use our eyes to gauge how well we are doing: the storms of life will blind us to the power of God. Every. Single. Time. Believe your Bible, not your eyesight. Believe what He says to be true in Jeremiah 29:11: "'I know the plans I have for you,' declares the LORD, 'plans to prosper you and not to harm you, plans to give you hope and a future.'" Don't let a verse you have perhaps heard many times before fail to hold the weight it deserves.

*Believe your Bible, not your eyesight.*

Either we believe what God says and live our lives built around it, or we build our lives on the often more dire physical symptoms. One of these two is riskier, and I'll let your own history help you decide about that.

Just remember as you decide: in the spiritual realm, eyesight is not required. In fact, this physical dependence hinders true sight. Peter found this out when he looked at the waves beneath his feet that took him down. Perhaps if you find yourself stuck waiting in Nowheresville, wrestling against the current difficulty, you've been using your eyes for a map.

Or maybe you've been buying into those negative assumptions

Satan's been feeding you. If you're a believer in Jesus, Satan doesn't master your mind, but he can throw things into it if you aren't proactive. That's why Ephesians 6:16 cautions us to "hold up the shield of faith to stop the fiery arrows of the devil" (NLT). Don't underestimate the power of negative assumptions.

It's like this:

$$\frac{\begin{array}{r} \text{Circumstances} \\ + \quad \text{Negative Assumptions} \end{array}}{\text{Faulty Conclusions}}$$

These assumptions have the power to derail a wavering faith. If we've got any simmering frustrations, Satan can fire a few gasoline-soaked negative-assumption arrows into them to ensure a fiery explosion.

Sadly, we see this damage happen even to ministry leaders. Negative assumptions lead to faulty conclusions. *People are against me. I'm alone and everything is up to me. I can't be honest about my stress.* Soon deep discouragement sets in. Often rash decisions follow.

*Negative assumptions lead to faulty conclusions.*

It's our pattern. Circumstances plus negative assumptions lead to faulty conclusions.

We come to faulty conclusions about relationships without knowing all the facts: They never texted me back. I must have done something to offend them.

Conclusions about our health: My leg hurts. It's probably a blood clot.

Conclusions about our future: I've had such bad luck in the past in this area. I doubt anything good will happen.

We come to faulty conclusions about how God views us: He

doesn't love me or think I'm worthy. He's decided we wouldn't make good parents. He prefers to use that other person.

If you believe that about God, it's time to get to know Him better. He wants you to know how He really feels about you. He loves you. He wants a deep, abiding relationship with you. The real kind, where you communicate to Him your thoughts, feelings, and desires. And He wants you to understand that a relationship with the almighty, supernatural God will in many ways be different from a human relationship. It will require we go through periods when we may not hear from Him in the way we would like. When you begin to develop a closeness with the Lord, it stops a lot of that desperate grappling for answers and creates a deep bond of security instead.

The more we learn to trust Him, the less we will need to hear from Him on our terms. And the less we will be vulnerable to those fiery arrows.

## Two Final Game-Changing Insights

I've saved perhaps the most important words for the end of this chapter, so I'm glad you're still here. There are two game-changing insights we can use to flip the script on our frustration over waiting on something to happen and wanting it to happen right now.

The first has to do with something the Lord is teaching me in real time, about how to help with negative thoughts and assumptions when I can't see up the road. (If only I had this information back in those seminary days!)

1. Don't worry too early.

    My seventeen-year-old daughter stood in my bedroom one night, telling me about how *this thing* was so very awful, and she was sure that *one thing after another* was going to happen next . . . and before I knew it, she had projected all the way to the end of the year. Ten months in advance, she was completely and utterly defeated.

"Honey," I said. "Remember what happened last time you worried like this?" She nodded her head. We both remembered. She had stressed about something early, it had all worked out, and we had laughed about how she could have saved herself a stomach ulcer.

"There's something I do a lot, and I notice you do too," I said. "I think we worry about things too early. Consider working on this with me? Because I'm not convinced these things you're talking about will even happen."

This had been my own private bad habit for a long time. But when I began noticing the same trait in my daughter, the situation suddenly became more real. I didn't want that for her. I didn't want it for me. I now had a new vantage point for myself. Funny how seeing in someone else something you need to do yourself can nudge you to finally work on it.

I know none of us wants to waste precious time worrying chunks of our life away. I must be honest about what we already know: sometimes bad things *do* happen. Sometimes, because we live in a fallen world, hard things come. If we could prevent those things from coming by worrying about them, I'd be the first to sign on. But we all know we can't.

The other reality exists just as much: that many things we spend our time worrying about never come to pass. A lot of us struggle with this issue. If this is something you deal with, perhaps you would consider joining me and my daughter in not giving permission to our negative imagination anymore. (Works in progress, right? ☺)

In my own journey with this, I've found some help in the Bible:

"Do not be anxious about anything, but in every situation, by prayer and petition, with thanksgiving, present your requests to God" (Philippians 4:6).

I also believe worry is like fear, incurable this side of heaven, until we will finally shed this human body, yet manageable with the help of Christ. That reality can drive us to seek progress instead of perfection. As we make progress, we honor God and get better. With our driving goal always to become more like Christ, we don't need to worry that we will settle for fear or worry—that is simply an incompatible mindset for a Christ follower—even in our understanding of imperfect progress. Pre-worrying is completely unnecessary and something we *can* stop doing. It is 100 percent possible to stop traveling down mental roads that take us to dead ends.

> *Worry is like fear, incurable this side of heaven, until we will finally shed this human body, yet manageable with the help of Christ.*

2. Don't decide you cannot have joy until . . .

The perception of delayed joy is an epidemic in the waiting community. Too often we believe we cannot allow for joy *until* we know for sure that thing in the future is going to work out. Until then, we will defer our joy. We accept this miserable lifestyle.

We'll put off joy until the hard work in our jobs pays off . . . until we get to the next level of life . . . until the dream we've had for years for that fixer-upper bed-and-breakfast becomes a reality. *Then* we will finally be happy.

We think we cannot have joy until that next thing comes true. Sometimes we think we cannot wait one second more. Sometimes our pleading prayers are so guttural they scare us. God wants us to pray guttural prayers.

*Absolutely.* Pray this way for the things you want, and certainly things you need. But while you're praying your guts out, find joy in the interim as well. Don't have a contingency attached. It can change your motive. Gratitude without qualifications brings unfiltered joy. When we bring stipulations into it, we move from thankfulness to transaction. Waiting is an inevitability of life, so we need to grow accustomed to this way of life.

Even if we are worn down in the waiting, these two game changers may help us get us through, but they also help us grow strong in the process. This is how waiting goes from just being hard to being hard good. I know you're tired, and the idea of going on a joy hunt may not sound appealing, given your long to-do list. But how does not being consumed by the wait anymore sound?

Remember: with God, it is not work without goodness, so there will be payoff.

A few last thoughts.

Rather than wait for joy to come to you, pursue it. Instead of worrying too early, hand those hopes, dreams, and burdens over to God and let Him work. After all, we *don't know what we don't know.*

Find joy in the air you breathe. Fully functioning lungs and clean air aren't a given.

Wake up to all of your senses. The food you get to taste, smell, and share. The flowers and the crickets and the trees that sway in the breeze. Only a Genius could make this stuff up!

Think about the ocean. Even if you can't put your feet in the sand right now, you've heard, at least somewhere, the sound of crashing waves. (A noisemaker app can even give you that. ☺)

Remember the beauty of the mountains with their hats of snow that tip to the majesty of God in His beautiful handiwork.

Find joy in human connection—family, a neighbor, the nice

person you smile at every day at CVS, or the friend who moved away whom you can now at least connect with online.

Thank God He left you with people to experience life with, such as it is. Find joy in worshiping, with or without other believers. Sing, read the Bible, pray. Show you care about others in tangible ways. Care first, even if they don't care as much as you want them to. You'll still find joy in that. Find joy in reading. A good book is a simple joy not to be missed. We can indeed connect our hearts within the pages, as we're doing right now.

Don't wait on that phone call or text. *You* text. *You* call. *You* take someone flowers. *You* write an old-fashioned card. Be the friend you wish you had.

Support others. Don't wait for them to support you. And watch how you'll one day find yourself surrounded by calls and texts and cards and cheerleaders in your time of need. Find yourself, at the very least, with a heart full of joy. Watch. It happens. God is good at lavishing love down on us when we pour out sacrificially. We sit around and wait for the love we need, but so many times we receive it tenfold when we step out first, vulnerable.

> *Support others. Don't wait for them to support you.*

And for my friend who is waiting on even this: Take that road trip. Eat the good food. Check stuff off your bucket list. Launch new ideas. Use those talents and strengths.

Don't wait on an invitation. Show up, anyway.

Don't wait to live. If every other thing in this life went away and you never got a single thing you are waiting for right now, He would be enough.

CHAPTER 6

# making peace with life
# when it's brought loss

You are the fountain of life,
    the light by which we see.
—Psalm 36:9 (nlt)

My friend Beth will never look forward to pumpkin spice latte season the way a lot of us do.

Like most high school friends, Beth and I went our separate ways upon graduation, but we kept in touch periodically. I went to college and seminary, married, and moved to the Carolinas, while she remained in our hometown, eventually marrying Mike and having two kids.

We actually went further back than high school. We'd met in the sixth grade, when our family rolled into Springfield, Missouri, in yet another packed U-Haul, for my father to take yet another pastorate. She was one of my first friends at our small Christian school, and thirty years later she is one of my only remaining from this school. Like attracts like, and though we sometimes butted heads, Beth and I "got" each other. Fiery and fun-loving, neither of us minded sharing our opinions. We dated the same boys (sometimes, unbeknownst to us, at the same time—shame on him!), we were cheerleaders together, and I stood as a bridesmaid in her wedding.

Beth's father was a preacher like mine, so we had that in common too. Bill Muench was a character, and I remember well his easy laugh. That was another thing Beth and I shared—she and her dad were incredibly close. She related to and looked up to her father just as I related to my dad. So in the fall of 2002, when someone we both knew from Springfield told me Beth's dad had died in a plane crash, my heart broke for my friend.

I knew she would be devastated, and she was, understandably. Bill Muench, a man with such zest for life, gone much too soon. Little did Beth know this would not be her last heartbreaking loss.

Fast-forward sixteen years.

My phone rang while I was in Nashville, preparing for a meeting with a publisher. From across the miles, a mutual high school friend told me something that sent my knees to the carpet of my hotel room. Two days prior, Beth's beloved twenty-four-year-old son, Justin, had been killed in an accident on opening day of hunting season—one of his favorite days of the year.

I was in disbelief. Immediately I called Beth, once again under excruciating circumstances. This conversation was different, heavier than the one I'd had with her after the loss of her dad years earlier, riddled with tears, shock, and heartbreak. How could my friend have now lost two of the men she loved most?

I wouldn't have dared write this chapter without Beth. I told her that when I called to ask her if she'd consider helping me write it, knowing grief and loss deserved a place in this book. I honestly didn't know if she would say yes. But I learned a long time ago not to come into a tender space as an expert about something with which you have only limited experience. When you do not know the depth of a place, ask someone who does. Listen, and take very good notes.

I am so glad Beth said yes.

As I was poring over the written notes Beth provided for this chapter, some details emerged that were new to me. Both Beth's father and son died in the autumn. Suddenly I realized she would forever associate heartache and loss with a season that has long been my favorite—one that is filled with porch pumpkins, mums, and apple-cinnamon-scented candles. A stark reminder that even as some of us feel joy and elation, others feel sorrow at the same time—a daily human picture of holding hard and good.

My friend has known the depth of life that has brought loss. Her toughest mission since has been one that those who face loss well understand: to make peace with a life that has gone rogue. Remaining here, when the person you love is gone. Putting one foot in front of the other.

But it's not just that. It's continuing to go on living in a different way—a way that isn't physical. Not becoming another casualty in the wake of an enormous loss is quite a feat. How does one not drown in the ferocious waves of grief? Can giving everything you've emotionally got to keep going ever be enough to make life livable, let alone good?

These questions are much harder off the paper.

I know that I *don't know* Beth's kind of loss, and I think that's wise to acknowledge. This may sound contradictory when I've said in an earlier chapter not to rate pain, but in this case it's not about rating; it's about acknowledging the differences. Beth helped walk me through these differences in one of our candid conversations not long ago by sharing wisdom from Gerald Sittser's book *A Grace Disguised*.[1]

The loss of a parent, Beth explained, is a *loss of our past*. The loss of a spouse is a *loss of our present*. And the loss of a child is a *loss of our future*. No wonder parents who have lost a child groan in a way that shakes the earth. (Beth told me her prayers, two years out, are often groanings.) I can only imagine that the pain of a future without part of yourself would be like living with one foot in a grave. Abnormal, ongoing agony. As Beth said, "You learn to live life without the limb that was cut off, but life is never normal."

Someone is reading along and nodding. Tears may be falling out of your eyes because you know this pain all too well. You may have a story similar to Beth's, so you join in her particular groanings. You share a bond with kindreds who have had children go to heaven, whose deaths you would wish away, pray away, and get rid of as fast as you could if it were in your power. In your darkest nighttime fears, this was always the club you most dreaded winding up in. I just want you to know that every word of this part of the chapter is written with you in mind, knowing I don't know this depth of pain but deeply desire to respect it.

While I was at the funeral home making arrangements for Dad's burial, I got a text from a friend wanting to go to lunch. *I'd love to carry on with eating, but,* I thought but didn't say, *I'm picking out my dead father's casket right now.* Sometimes people just don't know. They can't. Even those who have journeyed through their own losses don't know yours.

Loss of a spouse. Loss of a parent. Loss of anyone we love hurts more than the best written words could ever express. Trying to put sorrow into sentences is trite. I know only what Beth and other honest friends who have dealt with deep grief have told me and my own experience of losing my dad. Relief remains a struggle. The words *new normal* become a dreaded catchphrase.

Grief is like a fingerprint, uniquely yours. Others can't know how that person smelled to you, know your private jokes, or remember what you miss the most. That private head-heart space belongs to you and God. Friends can't know how you need to cry and process, what words will help (or that none do, really), or whether you need them to stay away or come close. No one can reduce the human heart to a manual on how to go on without a part of us.

So I won't try to write one.

Instead, I will let Beth, who knows this particular groaning, speak into this from her heart and from her perspective. I am so grateful for her words.

> Grief and joy can exist in the same space. This is difficult to deal with at first. Your heart has grieved for so long that it feels disingenuous to be excited or happy about something. Our first granddaughter was born in June 2020. Collins has been the rainbow after the storm. The damage from the storm still exists, but God's blessings peek through.
>
> When life brings you loss, there is no way to pull yourself up. You can't rise to the occasion. Therefore, it is crucial to have a life built on a firm foundation. The peace comes in the things that we remember about God's faithfulness.
>
> I hold on tightly to this: there is more to life than is here on earth. I don't think I could have persevered without the belief that "nothing is wasted." Paul said in Philippians 1:12, "I want you to know, brothers, that what has happened to me has really served to advance the gospel" (ESV).
>
> Loss has changed me. It's not that I was unapproachable, but it has shown me how to be human.

The death of my father taught me that it is okay to ask God, "Why?" The death of Justin tested my ability to stand on my own two feet. I can't. Candidly, I honestly would have bypassed all this grief, loss, and heartache. There is a set of people who say that all of this happened "so that" God could use it. I don't see it that way. I believe Scripture teaches that God wants to use us and our lives to show others His power.

My last thoughts would be these two scriptures:

Though the fig tree does not bud and there are no grapes on the vines, though the olive crop fails and the fields produce no food, though there are no sheep in the pen and no cattle in the stalls, yet I will rejoice in the LORD, I will be joyful in God my Savior. (Habakkuk 3:17–18)

And we know that in all things God works for the good of those who love him, who have been called according to his purpose. (Romans 8:28)

To get to verse 28, you have to read and understand Romans 8:18–27. In a sin-cursed world, God is working our sufferings (verse 18), the groanings of all creation (verse 22), and our weakness (verse 26) together for His ultimate good. Verse 28 does not promise everything to be good. But with God, good comes from it. The seventeen hundred people who attended Justin's funeral. The players, team, families, coaches, and school administration we've had interactions with since.

That is my desire. That even in my weakness, others will be pointed to Christ.

That is the only way I can continue.

## Gaining Perspective

For some of us, it's not one big loss that marks our lives. It's loss after loss we've experienced that has led us to feel as though we constantly have a losing hand.

Our spouse leaves us. Our job falls through. We find a good church, and then it splits down the middle and leaves us without a spiritual home and looking for a new one—all over again. Just one of these hurts would be hard, but put them together and a combination of blows threatens to take us out. If I've learned one thing, it's that life doesn't ask permission to be hard.

Loss is hard because it's rarely on our terms. Otherwise, it would be choice, not loss. I've heard people say, "I didn't lose my loved one. I know where they are." And that is the truth: for a believer in Jesus, you don't really lose people when they leave this earth. But you certainly feel the hole left behind.

*Loss is hard because it's rarely on our terms.*

As novelist John Green once said, "It hurts because it mattered."[2] Loss supports this. It is a large reason we struggle with hurts from the church. Many of us are walking around with tough fronts, hiding deep wounds at the hands of our spiritual families, saying harsh things about the church. But, most of the time, that's the pain talking. We don't really hate the church. We love her. A hurt heart is often masked by extreme words. We miss what we've lost so much that it's easier to just be mad. We aren't mad at the church because she never mattered. We are mad because she did, wildly so. So much so, it broke our hearts.

Our people matter to us. The closer the relationship, the deeper the ache when it's lost.

Part of the ache might be regret. Sometimes we feel a deep loss because we weren't close, didn't say that one last I love you, wish we could have done or been more. Regret is one of those things that prolongs wounds and deters healing. That is when we have to remember those two words from chapter 1 that are so important in our process to get well: *What now?* The longer we keep hitting replay on what we wish were different, the longer we stay in a furnace of pain.

Part of grief is often anger. When loss takes from us, we get wildly fierce. In some cases, our anger turns inward, and we completely shut down. When we lose people, even if we did the walking away, we may be too mad to honor how much we once loved them. But when we are ready, it would do us some real good. If we could see that the depth to which we mourn a thing often reflects how *deeply* we once loved it, we might be able to plant flowers around its memory. Notice I didn't say length (how long we loved) or expression (the ways in which we loved) because time doesn't prove how much we loved a relationship, nor do the ways we express love prove its depth.

This may be hard to hear, especially during fresh grief, because loss makes us feel as if we're the most unfortunate people in the world. But, over time, God can help us see the blessing of having gone through it. A brief gift is still a gift. I am notorious for wanting things on my terms, which absolutely means not only the *things* I want but also for the length of time. God has had to remind me on many occasions that our relationship doesn't include me telling Him details and Him executing them. I still want this, by the way. But I am learning, slowly, that I can live without all my demands being met.

I know that asking you to consider making peace with your loss probably feels like a horrible idea when you never agreed with the loss in the first place.

I know you may be mad at your life, mad at God, or mad at the way things have turned out. Maybe all three.

What if the anger isn't really anger? What if it is love, turned to hurt? If that is true, could that love be directed into something hopeful?

What if staying away—from relationships or the outside world—isn't really because you don't like people? Could you love again, and lose, and trust that you will again, and be okay if you do?

You don't have to agree with your loss to make peace with it.

What I'm suggesting is, as part of our healing, we pray for God to change our perspective. Not only so we can simply stay alive to our life, but also so He can make *much* of our life. I know you may not believe that you have a lot left after your loss, so to hear that He can still do His greatest work in you seems like a reach. But I wholeheartedly believe that it is true. He can not only do this within His intention and capabilities, but it won't require us getting on board with something we can't agree with in theory. Perspective changes are not concessions. They are agreeing to possess a different outlook to help us press on while the reality of our circumstances stays the same.

*You don't have to agree with your loss to make peace with it.*

We can all do this, with the help of God.

Making peace when life brings loss doesn't mean we are ever okay with it. It means our only alternative to acceptance is to stop living too.

Making peace doesn't make the loss right. It decides not to waste the next years trying to undo something we don't have the power to undo.

Making peace isn't just going along with a plan that caused you pain and dramatically changed your life. It's choosing not to let the world steal away any more of your good life.

If we run to our Bibles when we are stripped of something we love, we often do one of two things. Either we run to the book of Job for comfort, or we run the other way because we don't want the reminder of how much worse things can get. Those of us who run to Job do so because we need to believe we can make it when the worst that could happen does. And, strangely, Job gives us hope. His life contains loss after loss, but He never loses God. For forty-two chapters, he goes on a journey to make peace with his life. Don't think Job did the journey perfectly. Otherwise, in Job 42 he would have no reason to repent. But somewhere along the way, God changed his perspective. All the loss, as hard as it was, *was* for the good.

Aaron had to watch his sons die right before his very eyes, according to Leviticus 10. Think he didn't have to somehow make peace with that? Hagar was cast out by her family when she was told to sleep with someone to bear his son, then turned away out of jealousy when she did. But the Lord stayed with her and loved her, regardless. Surely her whole story was something she had to make peace with (Genesis 16–21).

And Mary, the mother of Jesus, lost her Son in the cruelest way, to the cruelest crowd (see John 19). How would a mother in these circumstances ever be able to go on, let alone make peace with life without the supernatural strength of God?

I'm not asking you to like what happened. Or suggesting you should be okay with your loss. Instead of trying to understand it, consider asking God to give you eyes to see something about it you haven't yet been able to see.

Only with His vision will we gain a different perspective, and only with Him will we possibly find anything good.

## ❧ GOOD: ❧
## Your grief and disappointment will bring newfound belief that what remains must matter.

---

*The hardest peace you may ever have to make
is the peace you make with yourself.*

---

It's not about making peace with losing *them* or *that* but making peace with the person inside. Many times this is the byproduct of great loss or a series of losses.

*We miss who we were . . .*
before that relationship.
before that event that broke our heart.
before we became cynical and hardened, almost
unrecognizable to ourselves.

This matters a lot because we often believe that we are not whole if we lose parts of ourselves in the process of enduring hard things. But hard things *always* change us, even if not for the good. When we face loss, it is inevitable that we will never quite be the same. I don't want us to spend any more of our life trying to get the old us back. I want us to ask God to do much and even more than ever before with what remains of our life.

It *is* possible.

I think about the child I was before I was exposed to those hideous porn magazines with Meghan. That little girl had a mind untarnished by things she had no business knowing about.

I think about the person I might be if some of my church

experiences hadn't broken my trust. It took me years to unravel all the complications a few of the difficulties church people caused. It would be nice to have an untarnished relationship.

I think about what kind of wife I might have been if my past relationships hadn't wounded me. Before I felt I must become tough, protect myself in case my man one day decided I wasn't good enough, and I made my husband pay for things he had no hand in.

And I think about all the "used to be" stories I've heard from women over the years. Stories of how they used to be so strong or so happy or so sure of themselves, *until* this or that happened. Now much of their time is spent figuring out ways to get that old self back, or at least make peace with what's left.

Who do you long to get back?

It's hard when you lose yourself. But it's good when your loss helps you find more of God.

Maybe you lost "her," but the her you will find now will be stronger and more resilient.

Maybe she will be the same her as before, but she will now be more patient, more understanding, more willing to sit and linger and listen because she has learned not to take things for granted. Maybe a lot of things will be better with the new her, now that God has helped her find her way back again.

> *It's hard when you lose yourself. But it's good when your loss helps you find more of God.*

We can look at our losses as unredeemable negatives, or we can look at them as God's greatest work in us *at work now*: the ultimate in what remains mattering. Much of this will come down to the choice of perspective and whether we will let Him heal our hearts. If I hadn't seen those images with Meghan, I wouldn't be able to help some young woman reading this who was exposed to the same not to feel shame anymore because she will know she's not alone. If I hadn't been hurt by church experiences, I wouldn't have the insight to be able to speak into hard places others may not know or show that it's possible to come back around and become a passionate church advocate. If I hadn't struggled in a past relationship, I wouldn't be able to appreciate a good husband. I'm not accepting any of these things *that remain from what is left* perfectly. But I have made good progress through the years.

No matter your backstory, the time will come when you'll need to make peace with yourself. Either with who you are after life dealt you those hard things. Or with who God created you to be from the start. This may be your longest, hardest quest ever.

We talked in chapter 1 about these historic roots of accepting yourself: you'll never make peace with anything else in life if you don't start here. At some point a degree of underlying turmoil will emerge. Who God created us to be can be either our joy or our albatross, and we will live with whichever we hang around our necks.

> *Who God created us to be can be either our joy or our albatross, and we will live with whichever we hang around our necks.*

When we lose parts of ourselves, we often turn to other behaviors—some that stick with us for years if we aren't willing to ask God to heal us fully as only He can. This is why it is even more crucial that we learn to make peace with hard things, not only so God can use them for our good, but also so we don't become people we aren't, truly, but are emulating in our unresolved pain. Here are five I've found to be most typical:

- **THE MORPHER.** Because we received the message that who we were wasn't quite right, good, or wanted, we decided it was noble to squelch our personality to fit someone else's mold.

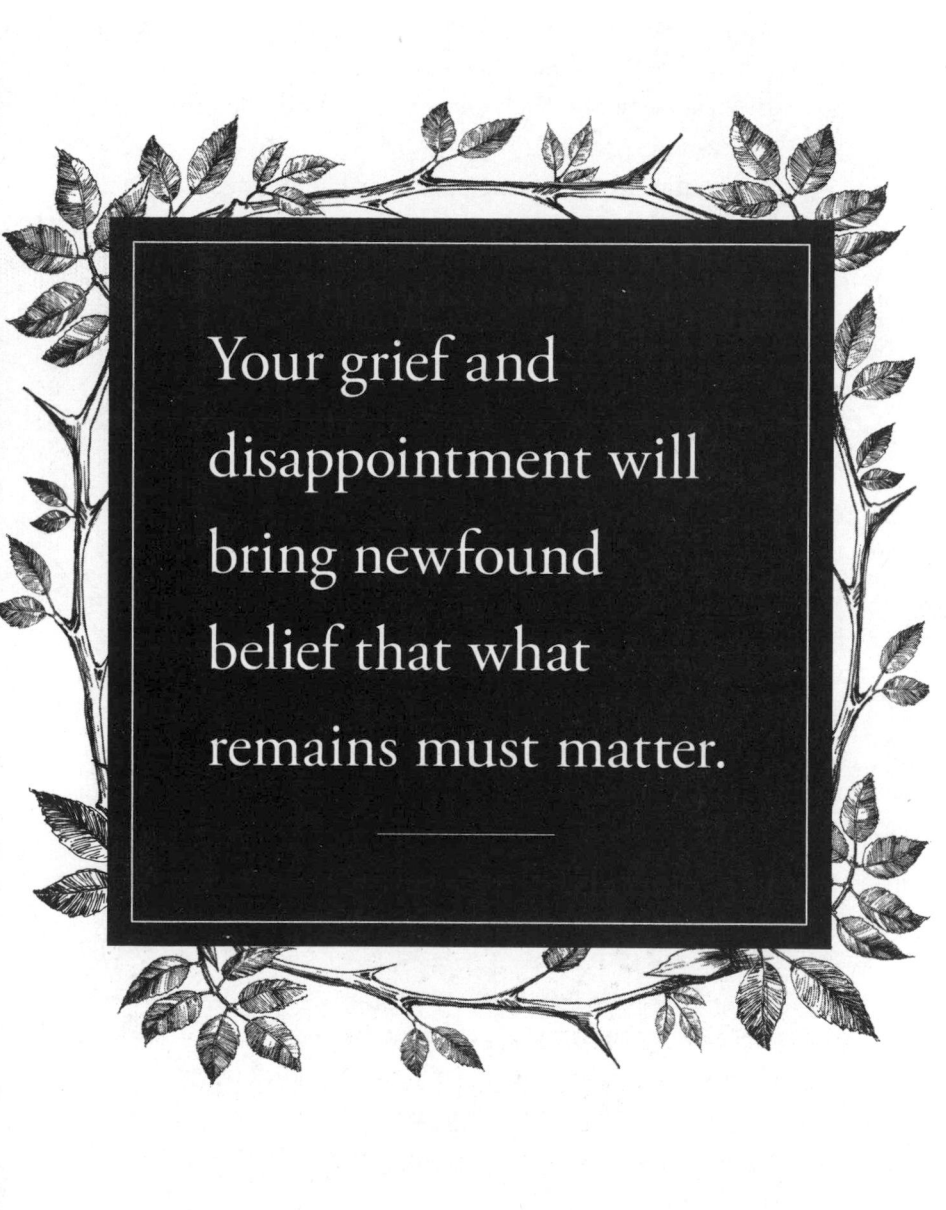

Your grief and disappointment will bring newfound belief that what remains must matter.

- **THE MUTED.** Someone abused us, and we felt they took away our voice.
- **THE ESCAPE ARTIST.** We got jaded or hurt and ran away or retreated to escape dealing with the pain.
- **THE BENCHWARMER.** We took ourselves out of the game due to insecurity.
- **THE HESITATOR.** We felt unappreciated and decided it wasn't worth the risk of putting ourselves out there again.

I'm well aware there's a lot of ground here—unspoken history, life lived, and stories—for us all, of which I cannot know. As you read, you may relate to the loss of a person or something else or the need to make peace with *you*. Whole stories are built upon tough childhoods and hard moments we'd prefer to forget. For many of us, a lot of pain, possibly a long history of identity issues, requires a lot of unearthing to be done. Whole lives are wrapped around narratives, true or false.

Please don't let your story or preferences get in the way of why God created you. He is in the business of taking the hardest story and making it end well. It may not be the fancy-bow conclusion, but it will close with celebration because don't we all really know the truth? All of this has always been about Him.

So the ending is good.

Making peace with life means making peace with the way life has turned out—things we've been an active participant in and things not caused by our own hands. I've watched a lot of us struggle with this aspect of ourselves mostly because forgiveness is often attached to making peace, and many of us are not so good at that. We either want to move on without true resolution or stay stuck in a stalemate with inner turmoil. Making peace is choosing to have a future rather than making more trips around the sun with the past.

## God Is Not Afraid of Your *Why*

Where were you the first time someone gave you permission to ask God *why*?

You may not be able to recall the exact moment, situation, or place, but my guess is you can remember the approximate time in your life because the discovery changed everything. The concept of being able to treat God as the approachable Father that He is, while still respecting His divinity, is a game changer for the Christian.

Some just treat Him as approachable and delete the reverence. This leads to a litany of issues resulting in a breakdown and crisis of faith. Others lean too heavily on God's holiness, misunderstanding His nurturing, sympathetic side. This leads to a compartmentalized, staunch view of God. Finding out that God accepts our questions, when they are rooted in an ultimate belief in Him and sincere desire to understand, makes all the difference in how we see our relationship, pursue conversation through prayer, and feel the freedom to be completely ourselves with our Maker.

Because I write mostly to the church, I approach the God relationship in this way. But I understand that this book may fall into the hands of someone who hasn't yet made that personal commitment to Him, so the questions may come before full belief in Jesus Christ. You may not yet have asked Him to be your Lord and Savior. We all have to start somewhere. C. S. Lewis said it best: "I know now, Lord, why you utter no answer. You are yourself the answer. Before your face questions die away. What other answer would suffice?"[3] All our questions ultimately lead to the one answer in Jesus Christ.

So ask God anything, friend, because He does not get offended, and I am confident He will be at the end of your search.

Just in case I'm writing to someone who hasn't yet received permission to ask God why, please take this as permission. (You don't need it from me or anyone else, but I know sometimes we'd like affirmation that it's okay.) The only way you may believe me is to try it yourself and see what happens. Watch Him not walk away or turn His back on you. Watch Him not be surprised. (He's God, and He already knows your thoughts.)

Beth told me that when her father died, she finally learned—as an adult with children—that she had permission to ask God why. To walk around for thirty years not knowing that, especially after being in church your whole life, that's incredibly sad. As a church, we can help disciple people better than that. When we don't know we can ask God why, we spend a lot of time asking other people, even ourselves, and we find a hollow result. Which is probably why we continue asking, searching in whatever vice—pills, alcohol, porn, food—we can find.

Asking God why may not ever result in an answer that satisfies you, but the process will lead you to His heart. And that may be the very thing that heals you from your need to know.

For many of us, like Beth, it takes an inexplicable life loss to find out we can ask God why. How will we make sense of a senseless tragedy? We must go straight to the One we know could have prevented it. Or at least we used to think so before we became angry and now aren't sure what we believe. We become very point-blank with our questions, maybe even literally banging our fists against a wall. *Why won't You heal my loved one? Why would You allow someone I love to suffer? Why in the world would You allow me to lose something [or someone] I love so much? Why would the world not need such a wonderful human when so many horrible humans are allowed to walk this earth? Why do bad things happen to good people?*

For months I begged God to heal my daddy and give him more years to live. When you watch a man become more than he has ever been on the inside, even while his body wastes away, you selfishly want more of this new and better version. Or maybe it's a noble desire. Either way, the prayers did not get answered, at least in the way I wanted. God did heal my father but not by leaving him on earth. He took him to his best life in heaven. My great loss was my father's great gain. As much as I want to be angry about it, questioning God, I've landed on at least one reason why.

It was better for my father in every single way.

The struggle I have is common—the struggle to be happy about what is better for someone else when it doesn't feel better for me.

Without question, heaven is better.

> "Never again will they hunger;
> never again will they thirst.
> The sun will not beat down on them,"
> nor any scorching heat.
> For the Lamb at the center of the throne
> will be their shepherd;
> "he will lead them to springs of living water."
> "And God will wipe away every tear from their eyes."
> (Revelation 7:16–17)

## How in the World It Could Be Good

I don't know any of the Old Testament prophets' Enneagram numbers, but they all seemed to share the same penchant for telling it as it was, not as they wanted us to see it. In a world full of loss, I often take comfort from the prophets, who had no reason to spin God to us or convince us that anything hard was good. Their lives weren't easy. They preached for years without success (Jeremiah), faced horrible endings (Isaiah), and clearly didn't enjoy a pain-free, success-oriented journey ("What misery is mine!" Micah 7:1).

But with every struggle the prophets had an uncanny sense of the goodness of God. Often they had no tangible proof He was as good as they were preaching, but there was clear belief behind that level of conviction. Even Micah, who spoke of his misery, in the same chapter spoke of spiritual reprieve: "For though I fall, I will rise again. Though I sit in darkness, the Lord will be my light" (7:8 NLT).

Here's how that type of belief plays out.

**THE PROPHETS SPOKE TO THEIR SOULS UNTIL THEY WERE CONVINCED GOD WAS GOOD.** David, as I mentioned earlier, made a practice of this. Speaking to our soul isn't merely sending positive vibes. It's repeating the truth of Scripture, as in Psalm 56:3, "When I am afraid, I put my trust in you," even when you don't *feel like trusting*. We do this so it will seep deep into the cracks where our emotions—anger, fear, and doubt, just to name a few—reside. When we are convinced our loss is not good, speaking to our soul works on those skeptical places. We may never feel like it—so don't wait on that—it is a *choice* not to die inside after we choose to live on. And at the very least (which is actually monumental), we will be convinced God is good. When we have a core belief that God is good, we will at some point come to believe that anything He allows isn't for nothing.

> *When we have a core belief that God is good, we will at some point come to believe that anything He allows isn't for nothing.*

**THE PROPHETS ACCEPTED THE BIG PICTURE.** Stephen is not an Old Testament prophet, but when he was being stoned in Acts 7, he knew it wasn't just about that moment—it was also about the eternal moments to come. It was about the bigger picture that God had purposed, which would include a mention in this book and many others, along with thousands of sermons, to illustrate this truth and encourage the body of Christ years later. This is why we can't decide what is for our best: We know very little. God knows the entire scope.

Jonah was a slow convert, but he eventually came around to accepting the big picture. As soon as he figured out his bailing on God's ask was the source of the storm the Lord had cooked up, Jonah got it. The lightbulb came on. And he made it right. You can read the whole story in Jonah 1–2 (I highly recommend it), but what you really need to know is Jonah's response after God's second ask, which is found in these eleven words in Jonah 3:3: "Jonah obeyed the word of the LORD and went to Nineveh." He preached there as God had asked him the first time. He accepted the big picture even in the frightening whale incident.

THE PROPHETS LEARNED THAT MAKING PEACE WITH THEIR CIRCUM-STANCES GAVE THEM BETTER LIVES. The Old Testament prophets didn't wait until their lives were good to preach God's message of hope. That is an important word for us who just read all about waiting in the last chapter. Despite any number of hard things, they lived with passion and purpose, more so than many of us who enjoy overwhelming abundance. We will never find contentment in our bank statement or possessions. We've proven it a million times over. And really, thank the Lord for no other solutions. Otherwise, we wouldn't ever find Him necessary. Our lack is what sends us into the arms of God.

Can I be completely honest with you?

I believe every single word of what I have written in this chapter. I am confident it is all true. Still, the weight of the losses represented here overwhelms me. Loss is real. Grief is permeating this world. Beth is my dear friend to this day, and every time I text her to tell her I am thinking of her, there is still a tinge of pain in our conversations.

> *Our lack is what sends us into the arms of God.*

And there is also the reminder of what remains: it is a new day, life still matters, and the best decision, no matter what, is to follow and trust God.

Amen.

# CHAPTER 7

# facing tough conversations and uncomfortable truths

The same sun which melts wax hardens clay.
And the same Gospel which melts some persons
to repentance hardens others in their sins.
—Charles H. Spurgeon[1]

When I was a teenager, my mom and I had a weird, accidental ritual. Whenever we went back-to-school shopping, or anytime she took me shopping, really, I would shop to my heart's content, without much restriction. Then I'd take all my fashion finds to the register, where she waited to pay, and quickly run off while the cost of my purchases was added up.

To her, it was a sweet show of caring and conscientiousness that I didn't want to know how much everything cost. I convinced myself of the same for years.

It wasn't until I had the perspective of age that I was willing to face the truth. I wasn't caring and conscientious enough to stop picking out clothes for my parents to foot the bill. I wasn't caring and conscientious enough to put anything back when I realized I might be spending too much of someone else's hard-earned money. I ran off simply because I didn't want to face reality—I was fine with spending the money, just not willing to hear what it cost. Running cutely off allowed me not to feel bad about something.

This created a pattern.

When I started dating and romantic relationships got hard, I would force a breakup by starting a relationship with one person while still dating another. College not fun anymore? I spent my entire freshman year doing not much else but gathering enough parking tickets to fill my trunk (a running family joke) simply because I didn't like the location of the parking spaces and skipping so many classes that I wound up with a whopping 1.8 GPA after my first semester. Coach too hard on me? I quit gymnastics around the third day despite his telling me I had a lot of talent. For many years I was a walking irony of deep grit and ready-to-quit when things didn't go my way.

It is only by the grace of God (and one crazy-committed husband) that I have not quit on my twenty-five-year marriage or this insanely hard writing career. During some seasons of each, not wanting to fail was enough. But mostly, over time, God compelled me to know that if I would let Him help me, He could break my bad habits.

Please don't slide by that point. Your toughest bad habit is not too tough for God.

My shopping game of deflection and finally facing the truth is important to us as we dive into the hard good of having hard conversations. This is where we often play cat-and-mouse games, in the church, in relationships, and even with God. We may mask the issues that make us run away from dealing with important growth places, with things like false nobility. (Remember how sweet and conscientious I was not to want to hear the total of the bill I had racked up?) We may deflect from them with insincere calls to prayer. (Prayer remains the first and best change agent, but we can misuse and diminish it when we use it to support our comfortable Christianity.) But we must get honest and be willing to be open—or God can't do the work in us He wants.

I acknowledge that abandoning comfortable patterns isn't at the top of our to-do list, but those patterns haven't really worked for us. Deflection is the biggest liar because it continues to add to a tab that eventually we *will* have to pay. Skipping school felt great until that 1.8 GPA. Those parking tickets eventually did come due, and they weren't cheap. My poor shopping habits— without me learning how to properly say no to myself over things I thought I *had to have* while in the store (there was no online shopping)—caused me problems down the road. So while it may seem that it's much easier to walk away from facing something, I want to encourage you not to. A good life is one where frequent escapes are no longer necessary, not where we find better and even better escape routes.

I'm spending time to talk about this because our willingness to face tough conversations and uncomfortable truths is as important as the conversations themselves. I say this because we can't get to the conversations without this first step. If we continue to sidestep addressing things that make us feel uncomfortable, there is no progress. Conversely, if we are willing to be

*A good life is one where frequent escapes are no longer necessary, not where we find better and even better escape routes.*

vulnerable and honest, even when it hurts, we will be unafraid to talk about anything.

This is where the hard of this leads to good: we become more secure and confident and less apt to fight others out of our own insecurities and fears, even when people act foolish or out of turn.

I know that we do things based on motivation, so let me offer a few examples that might inspire you to react differently the next time you're called on to face an uncomfortable truth. If, for instance, you are able to sit around a table with people who look and believe differently than you do and no one leaves angry, even after a spirited conversation, this is a good payoff. It is also rare. Most of us don't find ourselves in this place enough, especially if we're the one who is historically angry in these situations. So when it's different, you'll know God has done a work in you, sticking in there and being Spirit led versus self-led.

If you are able to approach even the toughest critic on social media without the need to win, you're on your way to being in control of something that would normally control you. That is, again, an incredibly beautiful (and unique) way to live. It means you have the ability to know you are right on a subject and not have a compulsion to prove it. People who are in a lifestyle of truth-seeking, coupled with Holy Spirit humility, begin to have an incredible new way with words. They also have the uncanny ability to be sure they are right and stay quiet. (*Gasp*, but it's true.)

It is the same with truth-speaking. If we begin to gather confidence that we are wisely speaking out on social media, for instance, we do so without the same angst when we go to bed at night. It is something I get asked about frequently—how to know when to speak up in a volatile, opinionated culture. When we are in the habit of nondeflection—first with God about ourselves—the Holy

Spirit begins to help us maneuver what were once difficult waters (impossible waters, I dare say, these days without Him). You can't create an internet course for that.

The need to deflect is taken away more and more as we begin to walk in honest, Holy Spirit confidence, no longer worrying about someone's harsh words taking us down, us not being able to withstand an argument, or someone finding out we are flawed and have no "room to talk" on some subject. Confidence and strength create more confidence and strength.

Not everyone runs away from tough conversations because they're afraid. Some of us don't like feeling restricted, and facing uncomfortable truths feels as if we are trapped in a conflict we have been trying our whole lives to avoid. The problem is we do far more damage in this process because avoidance breeds resentment and secrecy. The church does not need any more of these things. In that way, we really have no choice but to face what we need to face.

You might be like a lot of us right now, looking at the body of Christ and wondering how we got so fractured. There are multiple reasons for this, all of which include our collective humanity, which is apt to cause problems all the way around. No matter how the problems started, certainly some of the division in the body of Christ has worsened because of a breakdown in conversations that have not been Holy Spirit–led but were self-focused or because of years of unconfronted conversations that are long overdue and have built up hurt and resentment. Do we believe the Lord can help us have better, more Spirit-led conversations? Do we believe God can help bridge gaps that have made it easier to avoid hard conversations in the past? I absolutely do. Because the Lord can do anything. But we have to trust Him to do it, ask Him to do it, and be willing to allow Him to prove He can.

## Silencing Your Fear, Not People

Instead of silencing tough conversations, let's pray to silence our fear of taking them on.

What we most need is courage because the opportunity for volatility isn't going to stop anytime soon in a clashing culture. Free will brings with it the gift of free opinion, so the risk for butting heads is high. But we can't hide behind excuses. No, it's not simply that we don't like that other person or that they are always unreasonable. No, it's not always that there is no point because we won't get anywhere, or that we don't want to open up a "can of worms." Sometimes those things may be true. But usually, somewhere deep down, we are afraid of something. It's just easier to blame it on anything other than our emotions.

Maybe we are afraid of losing connection with people we love. This is often true, especially when it comes to varying convictions or viewpoints. When we part ways with the theology in which we were raised, for example, we may be convinced that if we voice that, it will be met with an emotional excommunication from family or friends. And in some cases, we may have experienced that in the past, so we fear it for good reason.

Maybe we are afraid we won't know how to handle being pressed or confronted about something we don't know, like what Jesus really says about a current issue—which is why it is crucial to know what you believe and, more importantly, why you believe it. The people who tend to get the most defensive usually don't feel comfortable in their convictions. Not the other way around.

We don't have to fear either of these things when we begin to create healthier dialogue. Healthier people have healthier dialogue, and those conversations continue to support and create even healthier people. So, in essence, having these difficult conversations and facing tough truths are gifts that keep on giving.

It becomes a cycle of wellness. When we form relationships (or recalibrate them if they are longer-term relationships that need adjustment) that are built on openness and trust instead of conditional acceptance based on conformity, our relationships become greatly enriched.

When we know what we believe, we are willing to hear people out, without cutting them off even if we disagree with them. More of this, please. This is something sorely lacking in this current culture, especially among Jesus followers who have every reason to be confident in what we believe. In this place, where we are open and yet grounded, we will have the wisdom to give consideration to someone's feelings, the humility to leave margin for the areas where we could be wrong, and the grace to honor an opposing voice even when we're sure they're incorrect. This is the epitome of spiritual maturity. It is something any of us who want it can have.

> *When we know what we believe, we are willing to hear people out, without cutting them off even if we disagree with them.*

I'm not asking you to water down your convictions. Society's opinions do not dictate Jesus followers' decisions. Therefore, do not waver because culture does not like your stance. There are certain things not a single soul can convince me to change that I believe the Bible teaches, despite the fact that society increasingly disagrees. But this is a help to me, not a hindrance. We are more able than ever to have hard conversations when, rather than carrying the burden to convince people of our position on an issue, we walk with the confidence that loving people and leading them to Jesus is our job. Don't confuse preaching a strong message with strong-arming unwisely. The latter doesn't work.

Let's talk social media, where this is increasingly applicable.

Some of our biggest fears project loudly in our comments on social media posts that make us uncomfortable. Except they don't come off as fear—they come off as arguments, mean-spirited and rude. And my personal favorite: critiques that include large doses of judgment from self-proclaimed experts of the Bible. I saw one of these the other day on a Bible study teacher's feed; she had quoted a secular novelist in a very innocent, inane post, and the rabid comments went wild:

"Shouldn't we be leading people to the Bible and not this man?" one attacked.

"Perhaps you should go back and study your Bible more before you give this kind of advice," wrote another sarcastically.

The air of snark and attitude of superiority might be what lead the tone, but underneath it all is an underlying, often unspoken fear: yet another Christian leader will fall prey to secular ideas (a reasonable concern). We are so afraid of this that we are willing to be rude to strangers through a keyboard. Our pride causes us to see nothing wrong with typing hurtful things to someone over the internet while enjoying an afternoon snack.

We can be better than ducking hard conversations . . . better than ambushing people in mean-spirited comments . . . better than letting fear drive us to live emotionally unhealthy lives and give Christians a bad name. This might not be the most fun conversations to have, but neither is it fun to live our lives in angst. These *are* fixable things. We *can* get better, yes, even over the internet. I think Satan has us believing we are doomed to a life of fighting with one another, but we are not.

Though social media has made this worse, our problems with people bringing up topics that make us uncomfortable are not new. Fear-driven pushback has been happening for a long time. When the racial tensions grew especially high in our country recently, I had friends who commented to me about how many followers they lost on social media when they spoke out on this important issue—to see racial reconciliation as the mandate of the gospel. It's not new for people to get angry over topics that threaten to rock their boats. I well remember when my father, an '80s preacher with strong convictions, did a hot-topics sermon series, from the pulpit (covering gambling, alcohol, abortion), and the mail that started coming to our home went nuts. One particular night the phone rang (back in the day of wall phones), and my daddy answered it. Cold chills ran up and down my spine as I heard my father say, "No, you won't," and "I will call the police." When I asked him what that was all about as he hung up, he just looked at me and said, "Don't worry about it, honey. People can act crazy." I went to bed that night terrified and wishing his sermon series was over.

We do not like to be made uncomfortable. You push on our level of comfort, and we will push right back.

Fear has us acting out in ways we never normally would. Even that person who called and threatened my father that night during his sermon series might well have been afraid of something. Or hurt by something in the past, which is also often the case. Dad hit a nerve by preaching on it, and that brought something unhealthy out. This is, again, why we have to deal with whatever we fear. We can't risk coming unhinged, leading to more problems.

The whole truth about the hard good—showing up when you want to shut down, not running away anymore so God can do His greatest work in you—is really all about letting God take you through an uncomfortable spiritual transformation process rather than you stopping it. Fear has likely been a huge factor in stifling your transformation in the past. Like me as a young shopper, when tough conversations and uncomfortable truths come up, maybe you walk to the other side of the room so you don't have to hear it.

You've decided it is easier to leave than to engage, easier to be quiet than to speak up. This is reactionary, by the way, too. Disengaging may feel like a relief, but it's not productive. It's also not spiritual. God wants to grow and change us, but He can't when we keep bailing out too soon.

One of the most important questions we will ever ask is this: What if we haven't known the good stuff because Jesus hasn't gotten us still enough to get us there? Really think about it and be honest. Hard conversations and facing truth certainly fall in that category. We grow up through this process—*hard* becoming *good*—because it takes maturity, self-control, listening, and caring—skills we aren't naturally good at when we're born. Sometimes sticking in and pushing through when we want to leave the room is maturity. Sometimes it's walking away from a heated or clearly unproductive conversation. But God will have to show us those moments, to be sure; and in order to discern what they are, we have to be walking closely with Him.

We each need to figure out our own currency and the whys behind some of the difficult conversations we've thus far been unwilling to have. I've had fears that kept me from truth and those private conversations with the Lord that could have been so important for my development, used by the Lord to draw me closer to Him. And yet I pushed them away because, at the time, they were too painful. Once again, the young girl living inside me, who used to shop and didn't want to hear the totals of what she had spent, didn't want to hear it.

As the Lord has been teaching me to sit in the uncomfortable process with Him, putting Him over even hard moments when I have to confront my own bias or long-running issues or sins in order to communicate with people well (sometimes people in my very own house!), here are some things He's been drawing me to see. I call them the Ten Best Nevers.

## TEN BEST NEVERS

1. Never fear the things that will be your best teachers.
2. Never fear all the *coulds* that haven't happened yet.
3. Never fear the hard moments that only make you better.
4. Never fear people who are human just like you.
5. Never fear experiences you don't know or share.
6. Never fear hard-to-swallow things that feed your soul with strength.
7. Never fear not knowing everything you feel you should already know.
8. Never fear saying the words "I'm sorry about that."
9. Never fear truth that will set you free.
10. Never fear things that can't change your relationship with Jesus.

I'm tender to us. With all my heart I love the faith community and want us to be better. I want us to be known for being the first to listen and care, all while standing firmly in our faith and unwavering convictions. Do you know, my dear friend, that perhaps even more than changing what we believe, the world actually wants something else? They want us to be better human beings so they can believe us about Jesus Christ. This is our massive breakdown.

True, some may stay angry because we do not conform. We are not promised acceptance in this world (John 15:18), another thing we often forget. But I have met far too many folks who just want us to be different in the best ways. Most of the time, we stand out for being the worst, not the best—such a mark on the gospel of Jesus Christ.

I am convinced that one of the ways we can turn this thing around is to stop lashing out, stonewalling, and running away from conversations that make us uncomfortable.

Especially when we benefit from silencing them.

God forgive us.


## Tough Conversations the Church Needs to Have

Let's dive into the challenges we face as the church—a group of imperfect humans who have been saved by faith in Jesus Christ. And by the way, I'm practicing what I preach right now because my instinct is to run away from this conversation. To be honest, I'm excited to write this section only so I can finish it and move on to the next.

Remember, it's okay to feel uncomfortable when you have a hard conversation. In fact, that's a sign you are doing the work.

*It's okay to feel uncomfortable when you have a hard conversation. In fact, that's a sign you are doing the work.*

Facing uncomfortable truths and having tough conversations are critical ways the church can begin to grow up from a self-focused immaturity and, as a result, become all that God intended. It's essentially the cumulative effect of God doing His greatest work in His people. It is also the way we, as individual members of it, mature in our independent belief systems and learn how to relate to others in more meaningful ways. We will all have to continue to do our own, separate work. And then we will all have to come together, more open, more willing, more reasonable, and talk (and listen!) to one another. Through practice, we'll not only become more and more willing to have hard conversations, but we'll also crave more true intimacy among our fellow believers, as is the Lord's design.

When we push through the uncomfortable, we develop holy habits.

Many hard conversations are documented in the Bible. Can you imagine how hard it was for Nathan to confront King David about his sin with Bathsheba? That was confrontational, for sure. Had it not been led by God, the conversation would likely have gone wrong.

This is a sign of a Holy Spirit–led conversation: the fruit it yields. I love what my wise friend Lisa Bevere says in her book *Godmothers*: "The goal of confrontation should always be restoration—not alienation."[2] Be looking for how your hard conversations go and watch for this sign—if it ultimately unites or divides—to know where you get off track. It won't be hard to tell. (This doesn't mean it won't be heated.)

Queen Esther had to have a tough conversation, to say the least, with her husband, King Xerxes. Lives were on the line, including hers. Was it worth having? Her courage saved the entire Jewish nation from death. To this day they still celebrate Purim in remembrance.

Paul called out Peter for hypocritically pleasing the Judaizers rather than upholding the gospel. Because of his fear of man, Peter did not want to be seen eating with Gentiles (a practice that certain Jewish groups still disapprove of today), and it caused him to literally jump up and move away from their table. Even though he previously had been eating with them, he now separated from them to show his visiting Jewish friends that he was still one of them (Galatians 2:11–14). I can only imagine how uncomfortable that conversation was. But allegiance to the kingdom demanded it.

Hard conversations among believers can't be about our egos (they'll make things messy), and they have to be about more than our feelings (culture has made these our god) or even our preferences (society's god number two) but always for the sake of the gospel. Without this motive, we get into opinionated wrestling matches. This is what is happening in record numbers right now, which is why many of us are choosing silence over speaking. I don't believe every Jesus follower lacks courage in their hesitancy not to engage with others. I believe Satan has made things so volatile and twisted that, to a great degree, it's created paralyzing fear and division. But we can't settle for that. We have to be unwilling to be manipulated by the evil one and give our egos, feelings, and preferences over to God to help us understand one another's situations and reach hearts.

We are notorious in the church for avoiding tough conversations. The outcry in the world often shows us the clearest picture of the issues the church has neglected to address and, thus, left the world without leadership. This is our job, church, and we must rise to it. Racial injustice is a clear issue we should be talking about, both inside and outside of the church, and, as a melting pot of God's creative design with a gospel mandate for unity, the church should be leading out in this. Not following sheepishly along. We need to be talking about our need for repentance. Our widespread issue of overt idolatry, lack of concern over human life (womb to tomb, and all stages in between, absolutely), Christian leadership celebrity culture, and the exaltation of men over God, including ourselves. We should be talking about sexuality and God's perfect design for sex within marriage and the important place women have in the church as leaders.

We should be talking about the Great Commission, which we have completely forgotten, and we should be talking about caring for our elderly and helping children who have been forgotten, abandoned, and abused. We should be talking about how we can be on the front lines of disasters, not just posting about them on social media but putting our hands and resources to work, helping on the ground. We should be talking about our lust problem, which isn't just about porn, and our gluttony problem, which isn't just about food. And we should be talking about how to keep our families together and strong and how to serve our families who are hurting and broken and how to help our communities and world find the one true hope, Jesus, whether or not that means they ever come to our particular church.

This isn't the full list of the conversations we avoid but need to be having, but it's a start. There are plenty of other things plaguing the church. The truth is we all have things on this list we care more about, and it's largely due to our personal experiences. But we don't get to pick and choose. The greater point here is this: *the church should be talking about things other people don't want to talk about.* We should be leading out in things, as the spiritual guides of this world. We should be the first to help in every situation. When things go wrong, people should look around and see the church front and center and say, "Of course the church is here."

And often, friends, *we are.* I love us. I'm not trying to make us feel better in the midst of a hard conversation, but I also want to tell the truth about the hard *and* the good. The truth is that the church, for all our flaws, is often right there, cleaning up wounds and nurturing back to health. Often we are not known figureheads but silent servants in the background. I see us. I've met us. I can almost always sense us when I meet us out somewhere. You too?

The whole point of this hard conversation we are having now is to get even better, so God can do in us His greatest

*In a tough culture, the church has prime opportunity to rise and shine bright.*

work in the days to come. I have that hope and belief. In a tough culture, the church has prime opportunity to rise and shine bright.

## ᔒ GOOD: ᔓ
### Your comfort will not be in hiding truth but in trusting God to help you face reality.

---

*I don't want you to be discouraged by this uncomfortable chapter.*

---

God truly can take the hard of this and bring so much good—to the body of Christ, to our relationships, and, personally, to us. He can use us in such a powerful way as we walk through this with courage. We can become the example to the world we were meant to be.

Often we get blamed for one or ten bad apples—sinners, like us, who behaved poorly and someone lumped the whole church in with them. God sees all that. And He works through us, despite it and despite us. I want you inspired to walk in the truth, no matter how hard it is, which will lead us to better health as a people and help us to be seen as the go-to resource for guidance and comfort in this world. Knowing we aren't the real hope, we are the tour guides that help people find their way to *the* hope, Jesus Christ. Wouldn't it be wonderful to have that reputation? I want that for us. I hope you do too. God can buoy our weak places, use us in more places than He is using us now, and turn things around.

As the world gets harder, people will need a spiritual compass more and more.

In the midst of this pandemic, my mother shared with me the most incredible story of a woman she recently met working in their

Your comfort will not
be in hiding truth but
in trusting God to
help you face reality.

tiny ranch-town hardware store. The woman opened up to Mom and let her know that she was terrified of getting the virus. Many people have shared that sentiment, panicked over illness as never before. She told my mother she'd been to church but hadn't felt much comfort there, to which my church-loving mother explained, "I'm so sorry that was your experience, but it's not really about a relationship with the church. It's about having a relationship with Jesus Christ."

The woman's eyes grew wide. "I wish someone would tell me how to have a relationship with Jesus Christ." My mother was more than happy to tell her and that very day led her to the Lord in a hardware aisle. Now, more than ever, people are hungry for hope. The church is needed more than we know.

Facing hard truths and uncomfortable conversations will allow us to be used by God in more powerful ways than ever. *For such a time as this.*

―――――――――――――――――― ജ ――――――――――――――――――

## Where to Go from Here

I like solutions. But more importantly, our God is a God of solutions.

It's good to see where we've been and even where we are, but what's most important is knowing where we need to go. Ready for some help and insight on how to navigate tough truths? Surely you didn't think I'd leave you hanging!

*Sharing hard truth isn't the same as a rant.*

Judging by our heated online interactions, a lot of us don't know the difference between speaking hard truth and a rant. But understanding that difference is going to be key as we move forward in a combative culture.

The mark of hard truth, led by the Holy Spirit, is that it is grounded and has a steady base. You might not agree with a hard truth at first, but you know it is not for lack of careful consideration and thought. You can hear it in the tone. (In Acts 20:19–32, Paul models how to speak hard truth to sisters and brothers in the body, from which we can gather great wisdom.)

Rants, however, are off the cuff and mostly reactionary. You can tell in their tone, too, almost right away. The reason a lot of us struggle to have influence on the internet, especially, is that many of our impassioned words lean toward rants. (Impassioned words, themselves, are not wrong. We can be passionate for good reason. We just aren't, always.) If we want our lives and relationships to move forward, to grow us to be more like Christ and be used for Him in this world, we have to stop ranting and ask God to give us the wisdom to share hard truth from the Word instead.

We may have only one good time to be heard by someone. We need to think very carefully: *Is this the thing I want to cash in my one good time to be heard on?*

*We get into problems when we give in to victim culture.*

There is a very real trend in today's culture of feeling persecuted anytime someone pushes back on us or disagrees with our position. I read a quote by Ralph Waldo Emerson recently that said it perfectly: "Let me never fall into the vulgar mistake of dreaming that I am persecuted whenever I am contradicted."[3] This is often where we live. We take on the mentality that we are victims of bullying and persecution, simply because people don't agree with us, which shows our self-interest. Moving forward, we need to take personal responsibility for our emotions and ask God to give us eyes to see real persecution (please research what is happening with truly persecuted Christians all over the world) and be better able to navigate conflict for ourselves.

*The need to be popular will compromise something eventually.*

I've written before about how our desire for popularity changes what we want, what we fight for, what we chase, and what conversations we are willing to have. In nearly every way, a desire to be popular will cancel out a desire to do important work that needs to be done in the kingdom of God.

What we need the most in facing uncomfortable truths is to have the heart for it—to pray for the desire to have hard conversations when necessary, and to move forward with them, even on the days they are hard. Facing the dialogue will change us, if in no other way but to help us get over ourselves. This brings on humility, a trait so many of us pray for and yet so often eludes us. You want to learn to be more humble? Sit with someone in a tough conversation for thirty minutes and let God chisel the pride off your heart.

> *A desire to be popular will cancel out a desire to do important work that needs to be done in the kingdom of God.*

Here are my ten best practices as we move forward. Please keep in mind that one size doesn't fit all, and prayer and discernment will be needed for every individual situation.

## TEN TIPS FOR HAVING A TOUGH CONVERSATION

1. **PRAY FIRST, ALWAYS.** Don't approach a meeting or conversation with someone if you haven't spent some time in prayer over it before you sit down to talk.

2. **CARE ENOUGH TO DO SOME PRIOR RESEARCH** on a subject you don't know much about before you come in. You don't need to come as an expert on any given subject. But you should care enough to have some working knowledge and

understanding of what you are discussing. Be honest about what you don't know.

3. **SHOW UP HUMBLE AND OPEN.** People sense an open and humble spirit (or its opposite).

4. **DISCERN AND DEFINE EXPECTATIONS BEFOREHAND IF POSSIBLE.** When people come into a conversation with an understanding of the purpose, you leave far less room for unmet expectations and frustration. A good practice is to take a third party with you when having a hard conversation—that is exercising biblical wisdom (see Matthew 18). But let the other person know you are bringing someone. Never blindside anyone.

5. **LISTEN MORE THAN YOU ARE NATURALLY INCLINED.** All of us want to be heard, and most of us struggle to listen well. But as we listen, we learn. And people feel valued in the process.

6. **DON'T LIE ABOUT ANYTHING,** but also don't say everything you feel. There is an important fine line here, and the Holy Spirit's wisdom and guidance are needed.

7. **DON'T BE AFRAID TO SCHEDULE A SECOND TALK AFTER PRO-CESSING.** Some people need more time to process through a conversation. Don't hesitate to say, "Let's cover some ground tonight, pray through it, and come back in a week or so and talk some more."

8. **FIND THE CORE OF YOUR HUMANITY AND MOSTLY CAMP THERE.** Finding the core where we can connect on a human level, despite divisive circumstances and differences, is crucial. Where do you relate? Make that your home base and come back there often.

9. **TELL THEM WHAT YOU THINK THEY SAID IN CASE THEY NEED TO CORRECT YOU**—clear up the facts versus assumptions. This tried-and-true counseling practice is so important. When

we speak back to people what we think we heard them say, we save ourselves so many misunderstandings.

10. **SEE THEM THROUGH THE LENS OF SOMEONE GOD DEARLY LOVES** and handle them as such. If we would view people in this way, we might well treat them differently. God takes seriously the way we treat His kids.

People are not ignorant, heretics, or (worst tag) *nonbelievers* just because they disagree with us. Too often we label people this way. If you've felt that way in the past, let God change your mind. Openness with others starts first with allowing God to do in you whatever He wants to do and work in you.

My best friend, Colleen, and I were having a conversation about something God was clearly telling me to do that involved having a hard conversation with another person. Based on my history with this person, I knew it might not go well and might not be well received. Also, I just flat out didn't want to do it.

> *Openness with others starts first with allowing God to do in you whatever He wants to do and work in you.*

The irony is that I had been wanting to become more humble and praying for God to help me develop that characteristic in my life. As with most things, He had the perfect solution, but I wasn't on board with His plans if they involved *this*. In the midst of our talk about what I was hoping to get out of this forthcoming hard talk, Colleen asked, "Why exactly are you having this conversation, again? Are you hoping [this person] will change?"

I stopped for a minute to think: *Is that what I hope? Do I want this person to change? Do I secretly desire some sort of retribution, recognition, or restoration?*

That was when I finally recognized what, in all honesty, I was seeking: *I'm not hoping [this person] will change. I'm praying I will so I'm no longer worried either way about what [this person] does.*

The ultimate goal is not that someone else will change but that you'll be okay if they never do. This is what the hard-good thing of facing hard truths and having uncomfortable conversations does for us.

Getting the upper hand or the last word isn't what will bring us joy. It is when we wake up and realize God has worked in us, and we don't need that kind of recognition anymore.

CHAPTER 8

# opening your heart again
# when it's been hurt

The way to despair is to refuse to
have any kind of experience.
—FLANNERY O'CONNOR[1]

IN 2010, I THINK I WAS DEPRESSED.

I have a hard time writing these words because I am not 100 percent sure I'm right. I never saw a doctor, and I was never diagnosed.
And the last thing I want to do is make anyone who has dealt with
real and ongoing depression feel as though I'm minimizing it by
playing a guessing game.

At the same time I want not to be afraid to call it what it was,
if, in fact, it was that. All I can tell you is what I remember. I was in
bed a lot that year, exhausted from exerting a fraction of the effort
my body normally handled just fine. Many days that's where my
kids found me when the carpool dropped them off after school. I

remember sometimes feeling ashamed but too tired to do anything about it. It wasn't my thyroid or any of the other physical reasons you become this kind of tired all the time.

One afternoon while I was still in my half-asleep, groggy state, my ten-year-old son came bounding into my bedroom after school. "Hi, Mom. What's up? Are you sick?" he asked, innocently.

*Am I sick?* I had wondered this before, but in a recent visit for a checkup, my doctor had assured me that the tests they did showed nothing physical was wrong. If this was some kind of tricky, undiagnosed illness, it had lasted for months and seemed to start, coincidentally, right about the same time we closed the church we started thirteen months earlier. Interesting timing.

"No, buddy. I think I'm just tired." This was the same speech I often gave the kids, so it rolled right off my tongue.

"Oh, yeah. I figured that, or you had a headache. You always get those." His words, so youthfully nonjudgmental, stung like a thousand bees. He was right. I'd suffered from migraines for years, but what really struck me was I had become *that mom*. That mom who always had the headaches. That mom who was always in bed when her children came home. That mom who was no good to anyone.

The Enemy of my soul hissed, *You are worth nothing to the people you love the very most.* I lay there crying many, many tears. I wanted so desperately to get out of bed. But I also *didn't want to.*

And even if I did, I truly didn't know how.

To this day I don't remember how I finally got up. I know that must be a terrible and potentially frustrating answer for the woman who is in bed right now, desperate for solutions. I respect us both enough not to make one up. I just know I did. All I can say is in every situation in which I have not known what to do, I have cried out to God. I've cried out to Him in the grocery store line. (In my heart, not out loud because no one wants to be a weirdo!) In the bathtub, over the sound of the running water. In my car. (What would we do without the privacy of our cars?) And, yes, when I couldn't get my head up off the pillow.

My memory is too hazy to tell you exactly what came next, but some days as God helped me, I was able to push myself through simple intentional practices like making the bed, leaving the room, and closing the door behind me. Some days God helped me get out of bed. And some days I stayed there. I believe with all my heart in the power of outside help—good counseling, the wise input of trusted family and friends, and medication as needed. I also believe God heals us from the inside out and is unequivocally the ultimate Healer. The two kinds of helps, professional and spiritual, often work together, another example of holding two truths (you can take medicine and also trust God), but I didn't have the energy, motivation, or money to go to counseling at the time.

If it's possible to become situationally depressed, that is what I believe happened to me from all the months of being strong for my husband while he struggled with closing our church. From holding everything together for our kids. From trying to show strong leadership in ministry. This is a massive risk for people like me who don't ask for help and struggle with admitting pain but *just keep going*. But it wasn't just that. My past baggage from the church had come back to haunt me, causing a visceral shutdown reaction. When we don't deal with our brokenheartedness, it leads to more woundedness. I had stuffed down so much hurt that I wound up in bed.

*When we don't deal with our brokenheartedness, it leads to more woundedness.*

If we're to have any chance of opening up our hearts again, we will first have to tend to the places we've been wounded. We'll need to be honest about them, call them exactly what they are, and let God do the soul surgery required for us to move forward. We'll need to become aware of our go-to coping methods and exchange some of them for healthier habits. And we'll have to lean into our faith on a whole new level—which is always God's goal for us.

You may ask, "Can't I live with a heart that isn't open? Must I go there?"

My answer would be yes and no. Yes, in the sense that many people go through life with closed hearts, and many die that way. You've probably known some. They may not say their hearts are closed, but you hear it in their distrust of people, in their anger, in their cynicism. Closed-hearted people see the world dimly. You may have experienced this firsthand when someone unloaded their angst on you or took something out on you unfairly. You've probably heard it said, "If you don't heal what hurt you, you will bleed on people who didn't cut you."

What hurt *you*?

Have you ever healed from it?

Or are you walking around bleeding on people who didn't cut you?

It isn't hard for people to notice when we are carrying old hurts from the church, for instance. Even when we say we simply "chose to walk away," we are often still mad. Not every case is the same, of course, and these kinds of hurts are legit. (I well know.) But healed people are future-focused typically, and they don't wear that look of pain in their eyes.

So yes, you can live with a heart that isn't open. But you will pay the high price of a life that is not lived in the fullness of Christ. That translates in two ways: God not being able to accomplish His greatest work in you and you not loving your life as you could.

*It's hard to open back up a hurt heart, but it's harder to live with a chronically closed one.*

It's hard to open back up a hurt heart, but it's harder to live with a chronically closed one.

## Pain on Top of Pain

The first time I attended chapel as a first-year seminary student turned out to be my last.

It was a mere few months after my father's forced resignation from his big church, and I had gone back to school with a suitcase full of fresh pain. News of his impending indictment by the IRS for understating income had reached the leadership at my home church, and they no longer supported him. This led to his swift public and, first, private undoing. Some were longtime friends, people he had brought on staff—ones he had prayed with and whose families he had loved during their hard times. Perhaps it was about setting necessary boundaries for them; I'll never really know. Dad was not a saint, and I am sure he played a role in their personal decision to withhold even support through friendship. But no matter their motives, the sting of them turning their back on him at his lowest point caused Dad deep grief (he never got over). The deal was made: If he would resign and go quietly, the leadership would give him six months of severance pay. But the congregation was to be told it was his choice and not given any details. (The specifics about length of time, pay, and what to tell the congregation are given to the best of my recollection.)

I flew home from seminary, sitting in the front row in an act of solidarity with my family as Daddy delivered his resignation to the church. To the church family I had grown up in and loved right along with Daddy. The people he had fed spiritually all week, every week, for thirteen years. Baby dedications. Bedside hospital visits. Marriages. Graveside prayers. All of it now felt like hollow nothingness in the wake of a mandate that he simply disappear with a few parting words and a *poof* on a sticky summer Sunday night.

And then, just like that, it was over.

We got up, walked out as a family, drove home, and ate pizza. I'll never forget my father's face, standing in the kitchen looking partly relieved, partly broken into a million pieces.

These were the wounds I was nursing when I returned to campus and found myself in chapel on a day when I felt like I needed it. Stepping inside the theater-style auditorium, I made my way to a seat beside several of my friends. The music started, then a welcome and a prayer, then a grandiose introduction of our chapel speaker listing his many accolades. I knew church programming backward and forward. This had been my entire life. By the time the speaker took the stage, I was barely listening.

Then came the moment.

I'm guessing it was about ten to fifteen minutes into his message, based on the length of time it took me to draw my name in bubble letters on the paper in my lap and fill them in with patterns. I was finishing up my artwork when his words piqued my interest—something about "not forgetting our first love." In good preacher form, he barely took a breath before launching smoothly into an illustration to solidify his point. Nearly three decades later, I can still hear his next words: *a well-known pastor in the Midwest.*

Inexplicably (aka Holy Spirit intuition), just from those seven words, I knew immediately he was talking about my dad.

I wasn't wrong.

My upper lip began to sweat in that way a body has of showing you it is paying close attention to something amiss happening inside your heart. Familiar details began to pour out of the speaker's mouth, some of which I caught like a cell phone with bad reception. *The pastor of a large church . . . lost it all in a scandal over money . . . left his first love . . . hurt a lot of people . . . don't be like him.*

I had heard many sermon illustrations preached by my father from many different pulpits. Now my life had become one. With all my might I resisted the urge to stand up and scream, "You don't know him! You don't know me! You don't know anything!"

Have you ever had a moment when you were furious but couldn't find your voice?

Instead, I sat paralyzed but for the blinking of my eyes as tears trickled into my lap. I've never felt so small in my life. No one wants to be *the story* when the story is that kind, told in that way.

*Not here too*, I thought to myself. If anywhere, spiritual walls should make me feel safe. Nothing quite prepares you to have your life reported like a segment of the six o'clock news to a thousand of your peers. Especially when you are blindsided. The trouble was our story *had been* on the evening news in our town, and now my already bruised heart was being reminded of that in the one place I had assumed there would be no judgment.

I'm sure the speaker's message was a good one. But good messages can't read a room, and there was one young woman in the audience nursing a very broken heart. No matter his intention, the speaker had broken it just a little bit more. (PS: He personally apologized to me a few days later when he found out I was in attendance.)

I've been told by people who remained in my beloved former church after we left that there was never another corporate mention of the faithful preacher of the gospel who delivered thousands of sermons as the once smaller church more than doubled in size. The visionary leader who had the foresight to lead the church to move to an undeveloped location that became a prime spot in town, which now the church sits proudly on. Not one, not ever that I have heard of. Flawed leader, absolutely. And aren't we all? But (again with the two truths) we can acknowledge that a leader is flawed and also acknowledge that God has used them—and be grateful for that. One does not nullify the other. Being wise in holding this tension can be difficult, but pretending one or the other isn't true is devastating.

People often find it easier to simply make something hard go away rather than deal with not knowing what to do with it. But just because you send something away doesn't mean *it goes away*. In the aftermath of the resignation, this didn't go away for my father or for the church members left with questions, holes, and disillusionment (we heard from many) . . . and definitely not for me.

Saint Augustine wrote, "I have caught a glimpse of your splendour with a wounded heart," and this perfectly describes the dance I've had with the church—and with God through the years that have come after.[2]

So I know a bit about church hurts. I know about people hurts. And I also know about the importance of healing those hurt places and letting God redeem them. This is the whole point of going through hard things—it is also the determination we will need as we increasingly accumulate brokenness at the hands of other people, simply living in this world.

And we need to be honest about it. I am not a proponent for our past becoming our crutch or anything becoming a scapegoat. Lots of people live in a state of blame, but that only makes one person pay. At the same time there is a difference between being *honest* and being *dishonoring*, and too many of us support secrecy culture in the name of not being dishonoring. The two don't have to be the same.

But that is where, again, we need the Holy Spirit. From our initial wounding from something—to how we respond versus react—to the subsequent healing from it, and to the way we carry the scars from it and live accordingly in the future. We can't erase the hard things we've been through, and we shouldn't be ashamed of them either. Opening up our hearts, again, doesn't mean we don't have wise parameters in the how, who, and when we let in. It means we don't live closed off from future opportunities and possibilities because we aren't healed from our past. The goal is to be healthy—no matter what unhealthy people around us do—so we can begin to be more reliant on the Lord's instruction for what to do in every future situation.

He remains the best Help.

You may or may not relate to a church hurt or the need to open your heart to it again. We haven't walked each other's road. What I want you to consider is that Jesus can reopen any heart from any hurt, even one that seems irreversibly shut tight. If you're saying, "No really, this one is impossible," I get that. But it's not. And He can.

You may also still want more insight on this lingering question: "Are you saying I should open my heart back up to just anyone and everyone?" Due to a hurt inflicted by someone, you may be unsure about staying closed to them, whether you're being wise or unreasonable. I don't know your specific situation, so I can't answer that. There's a difference between being closed off to people in bitterness and wisely gating your time and emotional space with some people because it's necessary. You need the Holy Spirit to let you know who to open (or open back) up your heart. There are some people and relationships the heart needs to stay closed to for good reason, like for our mental health. God doesn't want us to stay bound in abusive situations in any way. I fully support having personal boundaries and concentrating our energy on life-giving relationships. At the same time I believe that too often we call something a boundary to justify our unwillingness to reconcile. We're unwilling to prod at that tender wound in order to get healthy. Only you and God can fully know where you are.

Where you are can be an indicator too. Pay close attention to how you are living your life to see if you are living in response to some type of pain. Here are four types of responses that are fairly common:

- **TORNADOING.** Sometimes we find ourselves never having dealt with a wound, and in the process we continue to incur other drama—like a pain cyclone that has us spinning around in constant turmoil. The root may be the original wound, but it has a tornado effect on our lives.

  Example: "She is always such a drama queen."

- **TORPEDOING.** Under-the-surface pain shoots out and hits others, catching them off guard. Often the thing that has hurt us lies below the surface where we've stuffed it. But it comes out at inopportune times, harming others with sharp words or actions.

  Example: "She is always lashing out."

- **TAILGATING.** Unremedied pain often hangs on and follows us wherever we go, like a constant companion. Our past hurt follows us into our new relationships, future jobs, and opportunities. It's always there, tagging along, causing problems.

  Example: "Trouble seems to follow her."

- **TORCHING.** Inflammatory pain ignites and burns things we love to the ground. Wounds from our past can become reinflamed quickly and ferociously, and people around us often don't understand why we get triggered and react.

  Example: "She's so touchy all the time."

These are the behaviors we often turn to as a byproduct of being stuck in a pain cycle. When we've been hurt, it frequently results in us closing off the valve to caring. It might begin with little things at first, like skipping that lunch date with a good friend.

Or not spending time on the hobby we most enjoy. Or avoiding a ministry opportunity. Before we know it, we can't get out of bed. One day we may wake up and not even recognize the person in the mirror, the woman we've become since we stopped caring.

I have reacted in all these ways at various times. I've gotten caught up in a cycle of drama in my college days by entering a string of bad relationships. I've lashed out at people when I felt especially raw and vulnerable. I've brought baggage from a hurtful romantic relationship into my marriage and made my husband spend unnecessary years trying to crack open a closed heart. I've incinerated relationships I cared about because I felt the other person had wounded me, and I was too prideful to deal with it.

We are all works in progress. Apart from God, none of us is who or where we want to be.

I don't blame you if you *feel* like not being open. But please don't. We are getting somewhere very good.

## Tending to the Hurt Places

None of us expects to wind up in bed.

We all want to live with joy.

We don't happen into hopelessness—we neglect ourselves there. We abandon dealing with hurt places and eventually it catches up to us.

*We don't happen into hopelessness—we neglect ourselves there.*

Please don't ignore those raw places left behind from the trauma of hard pages in your past. Ask God for courage to take the next step toward healing, so He can do His greatest work in you. It may even be those parts of your story He's waiting to leverage for His glory.

And keep this in mind: *not all parts of what hurt you and caused you to close up your heart may be used, or need to be, in your redemption story.*

Hold loosely what parts God wants to use. Don't try to make it all fit. Sometimes we make the mistake of believing if some parts still make no sense, or are too gross, none of it is redeemable. Let's let God decide. Some of those parts we deem scraps to be thrown away like potato peelings He will salvage and turn into a masterpiece that feeds the body with hope and strength. On the other hand, some of those parts we feel are the shiniest details of our redemption story might turn out to be just for us—to marvel at in our sweetest, most intimate moments with Him. Either way, none of this is about us. Our story is meant to shine a spotlight on His story, so let's trust Him with those details.

*Expect and be prepared to be triggered sometimes.* There are still times I have visceral reactions to certain things in church settings that do not bother anyone else. Several years ago we were doing a recitation of some kind, a repeat-this-after-me situation, and I refused to do it. My lips literally wouldn't move. I still struggle with this because it brings to mind stale and systematic programming, something I had to heal from in my religious background. In the same way, I can feel my heart start to close when a church service feels overly produced.

When it happens, I know to whisper to God, *It's You, it's always been You, and it will always be You, Jesus,* or something like that. Triggers can easily slide into judgment, and that creates unnecessary criticism and distrust. It can also block us from worship, community, and hearing the voice of God. Be prepared for your own triggers. Have a plan. Don't let them scare you away from trusting the Lord with your open heart. And, most of all, don't let triggers cause you to assume things you don't have the spiritual intel to know. Triggers often lead to assumptions. Let God do the job of managing motives. Just keep showing up to honor Him in all you do.

It is the key to your process of opening back up.

## ✌ GOOD: ⚗

**You will be free to live big in the imperfect but precious present without being kept small by a difficult past.**

---

*Redemption is a most glorious thing.*

---

When Daddy died, the Lord challenged me to use the things I learned from my lifelong relationship with the church for His glory.

At the grave, the very day I sat and listened to a trumpet play taps while my mom received a majestically folded flag before my father was laid into the earth, God spoke to my soul: *What are you going to do with all you know?* I was a bit taken aback at first, but at the same time I knew exactly what He meant. He didn't want more busyness out of me. He wanted me to use what I *lived*. All the things, both hard and good.

For more than forty years I had a front-row seat to what can happen when even the most well-intended servants of God don't tend to the broken places and just keep going. My dad needed a true spiritual reckoning all those years he poured out. He needed desperately to know God loved him as much as he preached it to a hungry congregation. He needed to stop and tend to the lies, the shame, and the broken places of his past, self-inflicted and otherwise. His wounds, gaping, came out in so many self-destructive ways. I watched it many days—my favorite person in the world fighting within himself.

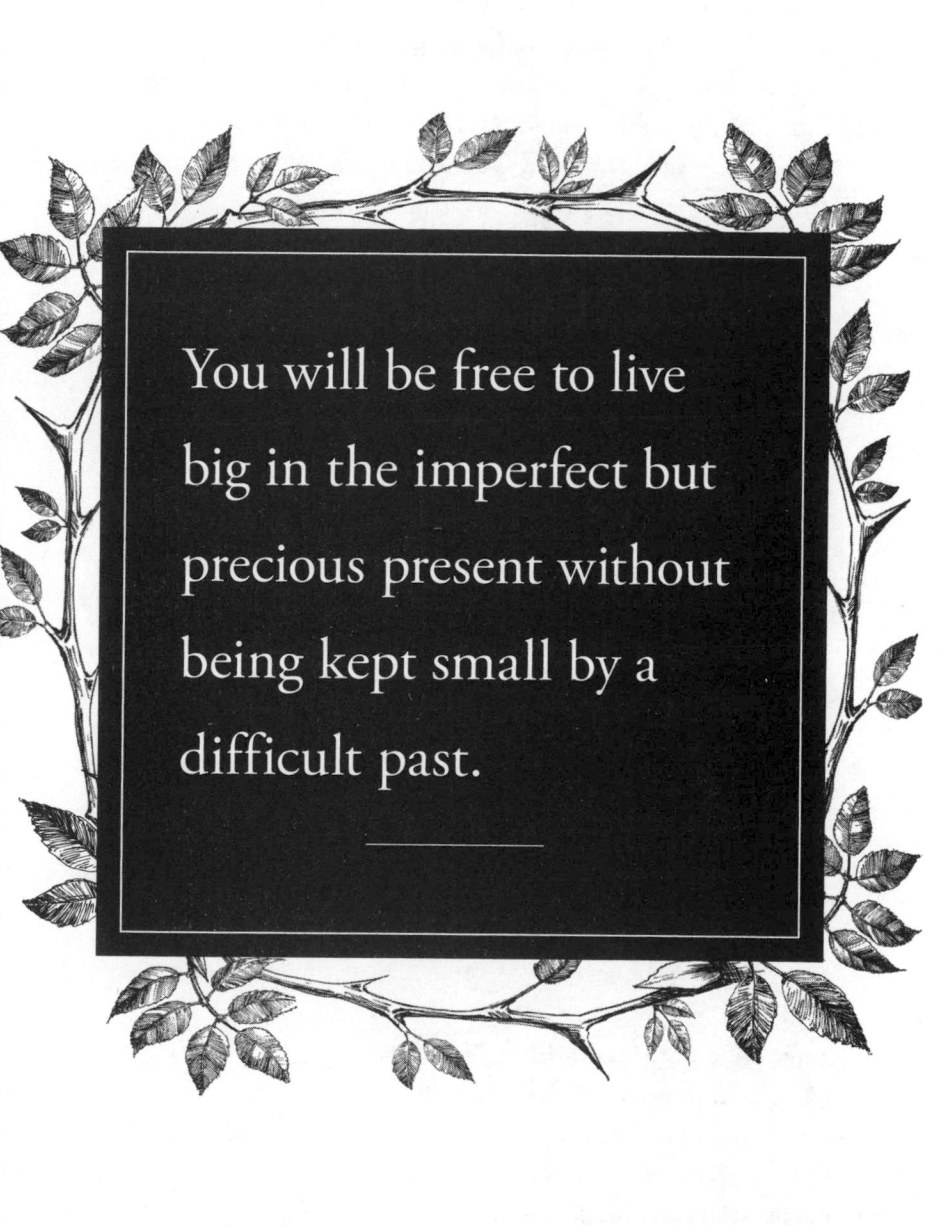

You will be free to live
big in the imperfect but
precious present without
being kept small by a
difficult past.

————————

Children might not know what to call a parent's internal battle, but we know it is something, and the something isn't right. I knew that insider stuff. I knew what it looked like to run away from the hard things, to react recklessly out of pain, to watch a life that God used powerfully—but could have used even more—have its influence cut short. I trusted God with my father's life, and I knew His appointment for eternity was right and on time. And I also knew God hadn't put me in a spot to see it just to hoard what I saw and learned. My own pain from riding the wave of his many hard experiences would—with God's help—help not only me but other believers not to fall prey to the same thing: a precious use of a broken vessel's history. In the end, that would be a gift he left here.

What about you? What are you doing with all you have seen and know to be true about God? How has He loved you through your pain?

After you answer those questions, circle back to this: *What now? What* can He use *now? What* will you do *now?*

A powerful way of opening your heart again is to completely give the next steps over to God. Hands *off.* And you might even want to sit on them if you're like me because what He uses to tend to the wounds may not be your first choice. But with Him you can always trust not only the results but the process.

## 1. He may use the thing that hurt you to heal you.

Letting God use what hurt you to heal you is the ultimate plot twist. In my experience, it is often the method He uses. Except with God, it's not actually a plot twist; it's His plan all along—to make good of the hard thing. "As for you, you meant evil against me, but God meant it for good, to bring it about that many people should be kept alive, as they are today" (Genesis 50:20 ESV). These were Joseph's words, for good reason. He spoke them to the same people who did him dirty—hated him, sold him to be a slave out of jealousy, disregarded his life. And yet God used those same actions to prosper Joseph and then help his family who had so wounded him in the past. The epitome of full circle. The definition of God healing with the very thing that wounded. Hard good, in every way.

*Letting God use what hurt you to heal you is the ultimate plot twist.*

Joseph had to open up his heart again after it had been hurt by the very same people. Only God could have helped him do that. We aren't strong enough to pry open a closed heart. That takes more strength than we will ever, of ourselves, have.

God alone has healed me where the church has hurt me. And He has used the church to do it. I don't know all His reasons for doing this, but I do know that when He uses the thing that hurts you to help heal you, though the scar doesn't go away, the pain from the wound permanently does. Redemption helps to close a wound and makes for a more thorough healing. And in many cases, as with mine, it also makes that place your deepest love and place of ministry.

*2. He may take you old-school through a stripped-down journey of trust and truth.*

One of the ways God has often helped me open back up to people is by reminding me that, at the end of the day, my trust really needed to be only in Him. This has been a powerful exhale for me, a person who struggles with historic betrayals. For many of us, opening our hearts back up, allowing ourselves to be wounded again, feels like the foolish choice. So we need to take people off the table when it comes to looking for stability. That role is God's, the One who can be trusted with our hearts even when people mishandle them. Please let that sink in. If we let Him be the end-all, be-all, and not other humans, our healing

> *[God] can be trusted with our hearts even when people mishandle them.*

is unconditional. It also frees us to love people for who they are and not be disappointed when they aren't more. God will often use Scripture to remind me of the most basic truths: God is love (1 John 4:16). God loves me (John 3:16). God won't betray my trust (2 Timothy 2:13). It may sound simple and old-school, but it keeps changing my life. I can open my heart back up when I know He is going to hold it and not someone else.

### 3. He may take you down backroads of remembrance.

Eight years ago God showed me the most powerful practice of remembering Him. Revelation 2:4–5 became a personal wake-up call: "You don't love me or each other as you did at first! Look how far you have fallen!" (NLT). And Psalm 142:5 became an anchoring verse: "Then I pray to you, O LORD. I say, 'You are my place of refuge. You are all I really want in life'" (NLT). The two go hand in hand—when we remember God, we want God. And as a result of wanting God, we run to Him for all things.

This is crucial because people begin to lessen, and He begins to increase. For us to have the ability to open up our hearts again, we have to have firm grounding in Jesus. When He is number one, we live with a different level of security and peace. It all starts with remembrance of who He is and how incredible He is.

If you are struggling today with opening your heart back up, ask yourself this question: *When was the last time I spent a solid hour just thinking about God?* Try it now. Get out a notebook and write down everything you remember about you and God for as many years as you've known Him. Start with God and watch your heart open up without having to force it. That's what freedom in unity with God brings.

All of this is to say: Opening our hearts back up really has nothing to do with other people. It has everything to do with how much we believe God. If we believe He has us, loves us, and can be trusted, we can live without the fear that holds us back.

And be well aware: Satan will fight you every step of the way to stay closed off because it's in his best interest to do so. It is not because he cares about you. He fights hard to get you to stay mad and unrelenting because then you are less kingdom-focused. He wins when you do not allow God to redeem your difficulties and see them become your greatest places of ministry. So don't be caught off guard when the advice you often hear popping into your head is to keep your heart shut.

This year my daughter is a senior in high school—the year of dreams and goals and all the things we looked forward to since kindergarten (or at least middle school). Turning eighteen, prom, seniority on campus, graduation, the cap and gown, and being "that grown." And this year, like many kids, she's attending school in the midst of a pandemic. Everything is wildly disappointing. School trips, canceled. Wearing a mask to school. Her junior prom was canceled due to the start of the pandemic, and no one can know yet if she will get one this year. It's a rite of passage, for goodness' sake, and not to waste a gown, she's thinking of taking pictures in her beautiful dress in our front yard. Everything is weird. She'll cheer with the rest of the squad on a sideline with no fans. Each day when something is taken away from her, my heart breaks a little more.

And I can see the risk of her heart closing a little more over the disappointment.

As her mother watching close by, I know I must help her rise above this disappointing moment because there will be many more in her life to come. And I also know these are the moments that cause long-running damaging belief systems to form: that people are to blame, the world is no good, and God doesn't care.

The other day I said to her after yet another disappointing blow, "Honey, I want you to know that if I don't make a big deal every time something happens this year or gets canceled, it's not because I don't think it's a big deal. It definitely is. It's a huge deal, and I'm so sorry about all of it. But if I don't say a lot every single time something else hard happens this year, it's because I don't want us to stay in a bad mental place. I want us to press on, no matter what. That is where we will find joy in our life amid things we can't control."

This is really the key: believing in Someone enough that we are truly okay no matter what.

*It won't be our loud efforts of performance that will lead people to Christ—it will be quiet perseverance.*

And know that, in that belief, God can wildly use us. People notice such a settled soul, especially in a world of chronic worriers. It won't be our loud efforts of performance that will lead people to Christ—it will be quiet perseverance. No one is ever truly moved by the thought of a perfect Christian. But they are moved by the testimony of the Christian who presses on. (Thank you, Paul and Philippians 3:13–15.) Whatever the hard thing was that has caused your heart to close or threatens to close it, God can help you be that testimony.

Do you trust God to open up your heart again? That is the crucial question.

## Steps Forward

Just as I began to do small things to be able to just get out of bed back in 2010, we can take small steps today, in the right direction, toward opening our hearts and keeping them open.

1. ACKNOWLEDGE (what you wish had been different)

   Recognize this practice from chapter 1? You already know how important it is to accept things you wish were something different, and you can't accept anything you don't first acknowledge. A lot of us, ironically, struggle to admit to ourselves what is hurting us maybe because we feel that in the admission, we make it come true. But these feelings about our circumstances are already true and acknowledging them actually has the opposite effect. In many ways bringing them into the light helps eliminate their shadows. They lose their power over us. What do you wish hadn't caused you pain? Admit it to yourself and to God.

2. ASSESS (where you are and where your pitfalls are)

   Where are you right now with your painful past? This, too, is important to admit. Articulate it, down to how it affects your daily life. You may well identify some ways in which you are operating that are responses to that old pain, things you would otherwise overlook.

3. KEEP GIVING IT TO GOD

   This is a vital practice. Notice I did not say it is a one-and-done because it isn't. You'll have to continue to give God your hard thing(s) over and over again, to stay healthy and aligned. The person who recognizes this stays well.

4. LIVE YOUR LIFE FORWARD

   Look forward to what God has for you! Whatever once

hurt you is a part of who you were and are today. Yes, it's still there. But that doesn't mean you should focus on it. Instead, ask God for all the exciting ways He wants to use the life that is still in front of you. The more you live your life forward, the less you will have time to look back and dwell on the past.

You have a life of great value. I want you to take care of it. *There's only one of you.* One chance to live with purpose and experience joy and happiness. Every time I learn that another person I know has cancer or has unexpectedly died in some sudden and tragic way, I'm reminded that life is indeed too short to leave here with a closed heart.

Or with time wasted on one.

## When You Will Know It Is Well

As I sit here today in my office, where I am surrounded by Bibles and books and all kinds of other Jesus things, my eyes are wet with tears, remembering that day in seminary chapel. I am still that young woman, listening to our family being callously dragged through the mud and our story treated recklessly for everyone's ears to hear. My heart is still sensitive to that moment, and I won't ever forget it, even if God lets me live until I am very old. It marked my life profoundly.

A million times in the past I have wanted to never open up my heart again to the body of Christ. I've imagined walking away, slamming the door behind me, and never looking back. I've wondered, *What would life be like if I didn't go back to the place that hurt me?* And here's what I've realized: every time I give God a chance to redeem something I can't figure out how in the world to redeem, He does. So I just keep giving Him another chance.

And that redemption piece brings humility, by the way. A healthy dose of remembering our own ability to contribute to the pain of others helps in the healing of our own inability to trust. We *all* need Jesus to stop the wounding.

Jesus, and Jesus only, is the Way with this. You may hear a message in this world that if you just love yourself enough, or get into a seemingly healthy relationship, finally, with someone who is good, it will heal you. Do not believe a word of it. I don't care how good any of us are; none of us has the power to fix a heart we did not create. We didn't form the valves and ventricles. We didn't command it to pump blood. And we do not hold its fate in our hands. There is only One sovereign enough for this level of attention.

I don't doubt life has hurt you enough to close up that heart of yours, in one way or ten.

But I know there is no case too hard for your Creator. Put your hand over the left side of your chest right now. Feel that? It is a spoken word from God. Every beat of your heart is saying to you, *God loves you. God has you here for a reason. God wants to use your life.* That beating rhythm is on repeat, over and over again.

You will know you are well when that rhythm begins to show up in the way you respond to even the hard parts of life.

What if you moved forward with new belief that you can be okay, despite disappointments? What if you began to value your life differently, knowing God has your trust, not someone else?

I told you earlier you could live with a heart that's not open. You can. Even though I don't want you to.

And I also told you that you cannot. Because Jesus loves you, He compels you not to live in a constant mode of self-protection, hands up, always on the defensive. You cannot live with a closed heart and have the life you want.

But rest assured. God can handle your newly opened (or re-opened) heart.

# CHAPTER 9

## saying i'm sorry first

To forgive, we set a prisoner free and discover
that the prisoner we set free is us.
—LEWIS B. SMEDES[1]

I DID NOT WANT TO APOLOGIZE.

For one thing, I didn't feel like I'd done anything *that* wrong. Becca (not her real name) had done far more wrong to me, from my vantage point. I knew if I told any of my people the story, they would side with me. I *had* told a few girlfriends, and the ones who heard details agreed I was the one who was owed the apology.

The problem was Jesus does not always see things the same way I do.

The other problem was, based on history, I was pretty sure I was never going to get that apology.

I'm sure you are curious about the details, but they really aren't as important as you may think. Just imagine any scenario between two Christian women, caught up in their own perspectives of a situation, where feelings were hurt with no clear-cut right or wrong, that Satan might hope would cause a misunderstanding of each other so the thing would fester, spread like wildfire, and from then on they would not get along.

What *was* important was how the situation was affecting me and how, at a certain point, I knew my withheld apology to this woman was not about the woman anymore. It had now turned into full-blown issues between God and me. Whatever Becca had done to warrant my feelings in the first place had now morphed into resentments of monumental proportion in my soul. Assumptions ran amuck. Hurt ran wild. Resulting behaviors, definitely on me. My thoughts were consumed with her. Why didn't she like me? My feelings were constantly bruised by my self-inflicted second-guessing.

I would get better for a time and then, without warning, get swept up in the emotions again. I have never been to prison, but I know quite well what an emotional jail cell feels like. This situation locked me up for quite a while.

After nearly a year of this soul turmoil, I finally decided to do what Jesus told me to do: tell her I was sorry. For what, I wasn't exactly sure. This did not, at first, sit well with me. Thus far, she had never shown remorse for how she'd hurt me or even so much as moved toward any type of communication. My pride wanted desperately for her to make the first move.

Some years later my forgiveness experience with Becca led me to write the following words in my book *5-Word Prayers*:

> Forgiveness is perhaps the greatest exercise of self-death a human will ever face. To open or reopen hearts that have been broken by injustice, to offer to another grace and love without their being worthy of it, is to deny our very flesh. When we forgive, we make ourselves vulnerable. We take a risk that the person will hurt us

again . . . that we will feel like we let someone off the hook when they should still be paying a price.[2]

Talk about an autobiography. I sure didn't hide it very well, did I? It wasn't hard to remember the feeling, the pain of making myself vulnerable to someone I was sure had the power to hurt me again. The trouble was it wasn't just about forgiving her. She hadn't even asked for that. It was about Jesus telling me to ask for forgiveness first. This was a whole other level of hard. Saying I was sorry when I wasn't convinced what to be sorry for was an exercise in trust that, once again, Jesus knew what was better for me than I knew myself.

But there was more to my resistance than the pain of apologizing. There was the other part too—the questioning part—that made me wonder if I really had to say yes to this hard task. The Lord eventually brought me to this conclusion: "Living with unforgiveness is a risk too—a risk that we will never have peace in our lives. This is, ironically, the higher risk."[3]

I realized that, with Becca, saying I'm sorry wasn't a far-fetched ask of the Lord—it was for my soul's sake since resentment toward her had taken ugly root over time. I was becoming emotionally hardened toward her. A chill ran up my spine whenever friends mentioned her name. I knew it wasn't normal. And I knew I needed to make things right with her, whatever it took, even if she never made her end right with me. That was between her and God.

But her lack of reciprocation would undoubtedly be the hardest part for me. When we can't control someone else's level of contrition, we often dismiss responsibility or downplay our own conviction. Humans like to check and double-check God's justice, just to make sure it's still working for us. And when it seems not to be, we wane in our willingness to do what's right.

The harmful thing about simmering negative emotions such as resentment and anger is that the other person who began as the target of your feelings ceases to become the main player in your process anymore. While the solution awaits—a saving apology—the person on the other end goes on with her life. Meanwhile, you're now dying on the inside. Please don't gloss over any part of that last sentence. Resentment and anger kill you from the inside out.

> *When we can't control someone else's level of contrition, we often dismiss responsibility or downplay our own conviction.*

Let me stop a moment right here knowing you may be struggling with these words. Maybe you've had a tough situation with someone, and my story with Becca is bringing up a lot of feelings for you. I get it. Nothing feels worse than an injustice, even ones done to ourselves. I know because—hi!—I relate. This is human nature.

But nothing quite moves us forward like bossing an injustice by taking back control from its grip. And that starts with making sense of what is actually happening.

Yes, I'm saying this isn't really about the other person. Even if it started out that way, a prolonged focus on a hurt has turned into something else.

No, I'm not saying you should apologize for what someone else did to you. You are responsible only for you, end of story.

I am suggesting you apologize to someone if the Lord prompts you, whether or not you share His enthusiasm. And I'm also suggesting that often, even when someone hurts us, unprovoked by us, we still wind up needing to apologize for where our heart journeys from there. (Why do I keep hearing my kids in my head saying, "But, Mom, he started it!"?) Blaming might be our favorite way of deflecting the pain of personal responsibility, but it ultimately delays the healing we truly want and need.

The practice of contrition, while exercised on a person, is an extension of our intimacy with God. We say I'm sorry to a person to reconnect with the Lord. That remembrance helps me because it doesn't require me to desire closeness to someone who hurt me.

It is what eventually led me to take that step with Becca.

The day arrived when Becca and I would be at the same place at the same time, and, trust me when I tell you, I wasn't that precious about moving forward with the apology when it came down to it. I can remember trying to get out of it, trying to convince the Lord she didn't even care and yet knowing it was His will it be done. And though my flesh was fighting, my spirit was in agreement. I'm so grateful to not only preach this truth but have experienced it to know of its reality: we can feel the weight of something hard at the same time we feel the assurance it is good and right.

The Lord didn't make saying I'm sorry easy on me. I had to pursue Becca, basically tracking her down like an animal stalking its prey, and corner her in a room so she would stand still long enough to receive the apology. (Sounds dramatic, and it kind of was, or maybe it just felt that way in the moment.) It was clear to me by her fidgeting, lack of eye contact, and scurrying around that she didn't want to be there any more than I did. And I still wanted to back out—of the room, literally. But I knew that the peace I sought would leave with me only if I went first. So I got over myself. I cleared my throat and stopped acting like a nervous middle school girl and said the two hardest words, *I'm sorry*. Despite my nerves and hesitation, I meant it.

If you think it was a beautiful Hallmark moment, you are wrong. Becca continued flitting around nervously, even after my apology. She avoided direct eye contact. Then she offered a rushed, half-hearted apology for something I felt sure she never truly felt but the weight of which I had carried around for a year like a ton of bricks.

And that was it, and that was that.

Saying we're sorry first may not bring us the redemption we hope and expect, but it will restore to us a sense of peace.

I left knowing I had done the right thing. More than that, I left with a weight off my shoulders. At the end of the day all you need to know when you do something hard is that it is what Jesus wants.

Yes, even saying you're sorry to someone who might also need to be the one apologizing to you.

## Why You Really Need to Do This

I need to tell you right off the bat that this won't be a typical chapter on forgiveness. There are whole books on the subject. Great books. Books written by some of my dear friends.

But there's a reason this chapter must be included: the life we want comes a through difficult process. I'm not good at saying I'm sorry, and I'm especially not good at saying it first. I suspect since we are all more alike than we are different, you struggle with it too. And yet, just because we aren't good at something does not mean it is not for us. I was a terrible cook when I first got married. Had I never cooked again after my first Hamburger Helper disaster, we'd have eaten out for twenty-five years. Had I stopped simply because I was bad at it or even because I didn't like it, my kids would have never gotten a home-cooked meal. Fill in your blank. This could go for a number of things that are good for us, but we aren't necessarily *good at*, especially at first. But as we practice things that are uncomfortable for us, we get better. We become:

- More flexible. A more open human is a more thriving human.
- More confident. When we do things we aren't good at, we prove to ourselves we can do hard things (with the help of God).
- More able. As we stretch ourselves, we grow in ability.

So the "I'll go first" apology is an important part of our growth.

It's also a discipline we need to get used to. It's something that will undoubtedly become more necessary as we live on this volatile earth—formative for us as Jesus followers. Maybe more than anything else, the humility that requires apology and contrition (and also results from it) shapes us into people who resemble Him. I want us to learn, together, how to do this hard-good thing so we can be an example to the world and ourselves of how God can help stubborn cases (like me!) find freedom in saying those humbling two words: *I'm sorry.* As we journey through life, we will need to become good at this process so we can fulfill the work God created for us to do on earth. Without our ability to acknowledge and own wrongdoings, God can never do in us all He wants to do.

We should learn to say I'm sorry first for our personal wellness and to fulfill God's great design for our lives.

> *Without our ability to acknowledge and own wrongdoings, God can never do in us all He wants to do.*

There's something else you should know. It is another case of holding two truths at once.

While being a firm advocate for the hard-good practice of apologizing first and immediately whenever God prompts, I'm *not* an advocate for apologizing for things for which we don't need to apologize. This is a different animal altogether, and, most of the time, this overapologizing behavior (saying I'm sorry in scenarios you don't need to apologize for, and you really aren't sorry for, but using these words to help ease tension in an awkward moment in a relationship) isn't really about being sorry. It is about controlling the narrative to gain approval of someone else. It is about self-esteem issues we mask as apologies because that feels less vulnerable. This chapter won't cover every single case of broken relationships or acts of contrition—victims don't owe perpetrators an apology for anything in their victimization, *the end*. There are one-sided situations where you truly don't need to apologize for anything. What I ask is that we pray and ask Jesus to help us be honest about what those are and be open and willing to hear whatever He says.

My hope and prayer is that God uses this chapter to encourage us to do this hard-good thing of leading out in apology in situations where we bear some responsibility, and yes, that includes the *even if* situations where someone has done something to us first that has then caused us to respond with resentment, anger, bitterness, gossip, and so forth. We are still responsible for those sins that outside wrongs have prompted. We can make it about who was the worst offender (I tried this with Becca, remember?), but in the end, it is about a personal desire to set ourselves free from the yoke of offense. Forgiveness is not a contest about who sinned worst. It is about who wants to be freed most.

Here's where this chapter will be of most help:

- Dealing with impasse relationships: where neither of you are willing to budge because you both think you're right
- Wanting to be set free regardless of what the other person does: when you're dealing with a person who is stubborn or in denial
- Knowing deep down you need to say you are sorry but truly don't know how

- Wanting to restore fellowship with God and suspecting the distance between you and Him has to do with your broken relationship with someone

If you find yourself in any of these places (or think you might in the future), the words in this chapter are most definitely for you. Stick with me. It's not easy for any of us.

## When You're at an Impasse

Here's what I know: the longer you wait to apologize to someone, the harder it will get.

I can be ready to apologize to my husband one minute, but if I wait two, I might talk myself out of it altogether. I will think of at least one thing he still owes me an apology for, and in scorekeeping I no longer feel obligation.

Just the other day I was feeling bad about the way I had gotten upset with my husband for something he had done and was completely in the mood to do a 180, apologize to him, and then (bonus!) even compliment him. But then he came home in a bad mood, said something to trigger me, and I took back all those internal warm, fuzzy feelings. No way was I going to apologize now. Over my dead body would I throw him a compliment after how he'd just acted to me. Likely, he was still inwardly upset over how I'd behaved toward him earlier in the day, and this was part of the reaction. And the cycle went on. *Impasse.* In twenty-five years it's a place we've been many times in our relationship.

Humans struggle greatly to be unselfish, which is why we spend a lot of time in relational logjams. Every time I think of that word, I can't help but think of when my parents lived in rural Tennessee when my kids were little. They had a creek running next to their house that was so pretty until someone threw a refrigerator in it somewhere downstream and it made its way onto their property, and nothing on the face of God's green earth could possibly get past. Complete impasse. Everything got backed up. It created a total mess, and until that big refrigerator was removed, no good flow was ever going to resume.

In a tension-filled world, with many people at impasses over this and that, I've been thinking lately about what it means to have the mind of Christ. This is what apology will require (among many other things). Without His mindset, I don't believe we can get there. It is incredible to me that we are even able to have His mind, but if I believe Philippians 2:5, I must believe it: "Let this mind be in you, which was also in Christ Jesus" (KJV). I love this suggestion that I can have His mind. If you read on to verses 7–8, you know exactly what kind of mind that is: "[He] made himself of no reputation, and took upon him the form of a servant, and was made in the likeness of men: And being found in fashion as a man, he humbled himself, and became obedient unto death, even the death of the cross" (KJV).

I adore all things about Jesus, but that He made Himself relatable to us in our struggles is one of the things I love the most. It was as if by His coming He preempted the nagging question we would have, *But what if this doesn't come natural for me?* by saying, *I understand, and yet I came so you would know that with My help you can do hard things.*

We have His mind by asking Him for it. We know what to ask Him for by learning from His example.

Jesus had a servant mindset, which means He relinquished His rights instead of fighting for them. This is completely countercultural. And yet, it was Jesus. To be willing to die on a cross, you are first willing to die to every other right. We have to die on our daily crosses too. What might happen in our relationships if we took seriously the command (did you realize it's a command, not a suggestion?) to have the same mindset as Christ? Think about that for a minute. (Insert your own scenario.) Would we still come to an impasse about who says I'm sorry first? Or would we find joy in being the one who models Jesus by stepping forward with the apology?

Consider the famous prayer at His point of death: "Father, forgive them; for they know not what they do" (Luke 23:34 KJV). This wasn't an apology to the people killing Him, but it was an apology *on their behalf,* which requires the same humble mindset and posture. To be willing to ask for an undeserved sparing of life at the same time someone is taking yours shows us that apologizing to someone first in an impasse situation is undoubtedly what Jesus would do.

I can hear the pushback now: *But what if they are wrong and I am right?*

Isn't that usually what we *all* think? That our perspective is the correct one?

There comes a moment when we have to decide if we are willing to push the refrigerator out of the way so water can flow again. Not just for the other person but for us too. If the Bible is true when it says that God's eyes roam the earth looking for a heart that is fully devoted to him (2 Chronicles 16:9), we can draw the correlation to restoration; a heart fully devoted to Him will also be restored to the body of Christ. Whoever desires God more will die to themselves first. Whoever wants a clean heart to worship will make the move. The person who knows they have done everything they can to make the relationship right is the person who will sleep best at night. In every way, it is better to say we are sorry than to say we are right.

> *Whoever desires God more will die to themselves first.*

I love what Beth Moore says to this. "Never underestimate the power of an apology. Few of us will want to pump our fists and cheer on our deathbeds, 'Woohoo! I never did say I was sorry for that!' The proud are so lonely. They won't admit it, but they are. No one's more alone than the one who views an apology as caving."[4]

When we find ourselves at an impasse, most often we are facing an issue of hanging on to a false narrative. It is typically one of three narratives we simply don't want to let go.

### 1. "They don't, won't, haven't, or aren't."

Some of our grievances against others are based on fact, but much of them are based on the power of negative assumptions (remember those from chapter 5?)—those thoughts and mental trails we go down that, actually, we've made up. We create entire false narratives based on negative assumptions, and before we know it, we are angry at people. This is where many breaches in relationships have begun. For example:

*She didn't answer my text. I guess I did something to offend her.*

*I haven't seen them at church. They've probably left the church.*

*He didn't come to the wedding. He obviously doesn't find our family important.*

This, in turn, keeps us at an impasse with other people because our grievances live mostly in our heads. The antidote for this is speaking into the nebulous *what ifs*—texting, calling, gathering truth in the form of information—and if there is a problem, getting it in the open to work it out. Then we have tangible proof to hold up to our negative assumption and say, "Nope. I know that's not true because (enter your proof you now know)."

## 2. "I can't."

Many times this false narrative runs us over, so even if we have a moment of desire to apologize to someone, we quickly retreat. We become like the sick man at the pool of Bethesda in John 5 who, when Jesus asked him if he wanted to get well, answered immediately with that same defeatist attitude: "'I can't, sir,' the sick man said, 'for I have no one to put me into the pool when the water bubbles up. Someone else always gets there ahead of me'" (v. 7 NLT). The truth is he couldn't heal himself (that was proven), and we can't either, so that reminder is important. We *can't* offer earnest, true, humble apologies to people in and of ourselves—that is incompatible with a self-preserving human nature. So in that way, the limitation is true. And yet, with the power of God, we can. (This is why, by the way, we cannot also believe the I-am-my-own-healer-rescuer-hero narrative so popular in our culture.) The *I can't* narrative lives in our disbelief of God's capabilities to overcome our human limitations. We are a stubborn and willful bunch, but tough cases do not frighten God. He's *resurrected human life*. So getting your heart to soften in an impasse situation—no matter how long that impasse has lasted—isn't His toughest case.

> *The* I can't *narrative lives in our disbelief of God's capabilities to overcome our human limitations.*

It's crucial that we pray for the Holy Spirit to help us have clear eyes to see the situation as it is and not how we have spun it. Have you said the words *I can't* to yourself when it comes to offering an apology? Have you believed you weren't capable (you're right) or that the power of God in and through you wasn't enough (not true)? If you've assumed the latter, please let this serve as a reminder that narrative is false. Put Him to the test. He won't disappoint.

*3. "They will."*

This is another negative assumption, but it's so powerful it deserves its own category. Deciding what someone will do before they do it is a dangerous move. It keeps us at an impasse. It has been my own personal downfall many times. I will often project what someone is going to do next, convinced that, based on their history or my assessment of them, I know their next move, *pre-move.* Sometimes I've been right. And just as many times, I've been wrong.

The trouble with this is, either way, we live with turmoil in our spirits and a broken relationship, often without provocation. So it just keeps heaping more and more hurt onto an already complicated situation. We decide that if we apologize to them for our resentment and anger toward them because of how they've handled us, they will assume we are letting them off the hook for their behavior, saying it was okay, or we want to be close again, perhaps. We may worry that, in this, we risk getting taken advantage of. But the truth is there is a difference between an apology and boundaries, and both are necessary. You can't control what someone thinks, but you can control how you behave. Don't let concern over someone else's actions keep you from doing what is right.

*Don't let concern over someone else's actions keep you from doing what is right.*

And finally, is your need to forgive yourself for something masking your need to forgive someone else? At first glance we may not notice that we sometimes have a sneaky deflection issue on our hands. Our unforgiveness of ourselves covers an unwillingness to extend an olive branch toward someone else. Everything flows from our view of how we see who we are and what we believe about a situation. I love what Jessica Simpson said in her memoir, *Open Book*: "I finally love who I am, and I can forgive who I was."⁵ Forgiving ourselves is so often the open door to restoration with everyone else.

## ೫ GOOD: ൫
### Your practice of first apology will turn a hurt heart into a healed and humble one.

*You can live well without that apology you may never get.*

Scrolling Pinterest one night, I came across a quote that blew me away: "I pray you heal from things no one ever apologized for."⁶ My mind immediately took me to three or four things I wanted healing from that, deep down, I knew I might never get apologies for. I would bet you have at least a few things like that yourself.

This is the goal: to heal from the wounds people cause, no matter what they choose to do. Just like me wanting to be okay, even if the person who hurt me in my past never changed. Determining to be set free, regardless of what the other person does, is the ultimate in interpersonal independence: we decide we don't want to be bound to anyone but God.

*Determining to be set free, regardless of what the other person does, is the ultimate in interpersonal independence: we decide we don't want to be bound to anyone but God.*

This is helpful in all things, since we can't control the actions of anyone, even those we may trust to never let us down. They remain human, so the risk is still there.

When you're dealing with a person who is stubborn or in denial, only God will be able to prick their conscience into action. Persuasion won't truly drive a human—it never has. At least, not in a lasting way. The things we want drive us, and God is at the root of all healthy desires.

*Can I own any part of this?* we must be willing to ask. *And if so, what part can I own?* Remember, it's not where it started or what the original offense was—you may well have not had a thing to do with that. But where is it now? And, even more, where is your heart now? Start there. Whoever understands this mentality of where it's gotten versus where it originated is the one who most often cracks the code to start dialogue and healing. Pride prevents the process of healing, and someone has to be willing to go first in breaking that down.

There is a very real possibility that you will never get the apology you need, want, and even deserve this side of heaven. But what I want you to know is that you can live with that. If you never get told I'm sorry, you can still say the words yourself. You can still live at peace with a person who does not acknowledge your forgiveness or your graciousness in apologizing. It can't kill you because pride being killed often hurts on the way down, but it results in double the strength to your life. We are weakened when we walk around with unresolved conflict. But a person who has slayed their pride can conquer most anything. Death to flesh results in abundance of life—that is God's equation.

*There is a very real possibility that you will never get the apology you need, want, and even deserve this side of heaven. But what I want you to know is that you can live with that.*

Some things will never be made right this side of heaven. Someone taking your loved one's life won't ever be made right on earth, no matter what punishment they've been mandated by law. My justice meter can barely stomach this reality. People getting away with abuse of all kinds . . . liars, cheaters, thieves . . . I cling to knowing that "God is just: He will pay back trouble to those who trouble you and give relief to you who are troubled, and to us as well. This will happen when the Lord Jesus is revealed from heaven in blazing fire with his powerful angels" (2 Thessalonians 1:6–7). Some days, when injustice feels especially heavy, I beg Jesus for this day.

We don't have to understand the how to believe it. We don't have to have a part in helping God stay good to His word. He's on it. We can rest.

I've lived with a disregarded apology, and it hurts. But we can also live without needing someone to embrace our apology or even acknowledge it. We die to the need for others to get on board with our apology when we trust God for the development of character that is at play in us through it. This is when hard turns to good. Count on Him to do what Paul said in Philippians 1:6 He will do: "I am certain that God, who began the good work within you, will continue his work until it is finally finished on the day when Christ Jesus returns" (NLT). He will complete this process of asking you to do something hard and then seeing you through to the good that develops on the other side of your obedience.

This can all be summed up in one word: *release.*

When we refuse to apologize, we are holding two prisoners— ourselves and someone else. The act of apology is the act of releasing both of us who are bound.

You may have never heard the Greek word *aphiemi*, but it's a word I hope you won't forget. I came across it as I was researching for this chapter, and it's a beautiful picture of this very aspect of obligation and release, the example of God as the purest picture.

In the New Testament, *aphiemi* spoke of releasing a prisoner or remitting a debt, but it also came to mean pardon or forgiveness.

Your practice of first apology will turn a hurt heart into a healed and humble one.

It means to remit, to release from guilt or penalty, as one would a financial debt, and is used to describe the voluntary release of a person or thing over which one has legal or actual control. It's a setting free. Later it came to include the release of someone from the obligation of marriage, or debt, or even a religious vow. In its final form it came to embrace the principle of release from punishment for some wrongdoing.[7]

When we look at this from a spiritual perspective, we see an even bigger picture at the cross—the act of Jesus physically giving Himself to fully cover for our sin, and when we choose to accept that, we then put ourselves under that provision and benefit. Yet another beautiful way Jesus is over everything, including us.

The cross is, indeed, a radical example of freedom and proof of how seriously our Father takes forgiveness. That Greek word *aphiemi*, meaning to set free, to let go, to release, to discharge or to liberate completely, is a verb that shows up 146 times in the New Testament. The interesting thing is the majority of the uses of this word express aspects other than what we think of with forgiveness: dismiss, release, leave, or abandon.[8]

I want to bring this to the very practical. Go with me, even if at first it feels silly. Take yourself to Starbucks (or even better: support a great local coffee shop!) someday soon and play out this scenario. First, sit in a place you can see customers walk in. Second, make a list of one or two (or ten) people you have issues with in your life—whether they know it or not. Third, as customers walk in, imagine them to be each of the people on your list.

As you "see" each person you have an issue with, say to yourself (in your mind): That is someone Jesus deeply loves. And then ask Jesus: Help me forgive (insert name).

It may not happen right away. Your heart may not feel automatically warm and fuzzy. But you have taken a hard, good step forward.

And as you do, remember these most important things:

- The greatest purpose of apology and forgiveness is to restore fellowship with Jesus.
- He went first so we would see a picture of what it is like to release people who don't deserve to be released, and know it is possible.
- Ultimately, whatever the grievance is that we are upset over is a debt that has already been paid by Jesus on the cross.
- We have to abandon a mindset of rights in order to be able to release the prisoner we hold hostage.
- Oftentimes that prisoner is us.

Not one bit of this is easy. Even as I type it, I don't like it any more than I ever have. But I know it is true. I know it is the way of release for us—to do the hard thing and come toward people with an apology, even one we offer them that we, too, deserve. I hold tight to the truth of James 4:10: "Humble yourselves before the Lord, and he will exalt you" (ESV). I need this assurance that as I release someone else, I release myself as well, and I release my heart from needing them to appreciate my apology. God and I know what it took to set both of us free.

---

## To Be Set Free

If you went to the Baptist church with me when I was a little girl, you would likely have come to hymn night, where number 144 was often requested by my eager friend Susan, a young lover of raising her hand to request hymns.

> *When I survey the wondrous cross*
> *On which the Prince of glory died,*
> *My richest gain I count but loss,*
> *And pour contempt on all my pride.*[9]

If the music director was feeling especially wild, we would sing all four stanzas and not skip over the third, which was always my favorite.

> *See from His head, His hands, His feet,*
> *Sorrow and love flow mingled down!*
> *Did e'er such love and sorrow meet,*
> *Or thorns compose so rich a crown?*[10]

Isaac Watts wrote the text for this incredible hymn—beautiful words that transport us to the moment of our Savior's ultimate sacrifice. When sung in a somber yet hopeful music key, it was as close to the real thing as we could get until Mel Gibson made the movie *The Passion of the Christ*. Even as a little girl I can remember *feeling* it down to my toes.

But as I've gotten older, I've come to appreciate the words of that third stanza far more. That "sorrow and love flow mingled down." If you know medical history, you know Jesus died of a broken heart, not as some may think from beatings and thorns and prolonged hanging on the cross. The Romans typically broke the kneecaps of crucified criminals so they would die faster from suffocation as they hung. But they didn't with Jesus. He was already dead when they got to Him. Not a bone would be broken because . . . *prophecy* (Psalm 34:20, John 19:33). The soldiers didn't even realize they were being supernaturally led in this way. When one of them thrust a spear between His second and third ribs, piercing his pericardium, blood and water physically flowed out, signaling His heart failure.[11]

Dying of a broken heart has the most incredible double meaning: what killed Him was also the greatest injury to His soul—the betrayal of so many friends. Please don't ever doubt that Jesus knows what it's like to be wounded so deeply. He knows, more than we ever will.

The words "sorrow and love flow mingled down" symbolize blood and water flowing out of His side, together—the great sorrow of paying this price in the face of such betrayal and hate along with His great love that constrained Him to hang there—the hard and the good. This hymn is about forgiveness. It is about love. It is about the release and the setting free. It is what Jesus is best about and always has been.

As you sit with your circumstances, there is no doubt that you have traveled a complex road. I am sure you have seen betrayals, and in those you find a small way to relate to our Lord's suffering. I am sure you have had moments of deep sorrow over a great love, and even while you held your grief, love flowed out of you in moments you could not contain. But the decision to follow the example of Christ in holding the hard and the good is the one that will make you most like Him. Because, in the words of the final stanza, He already gave it all. So we could have everything. And so everything that is hard for us would, through Him, be made possible.

> *Were the whole realm of nature mine,*
> *That were a present far too small;*
> *Love so amazing, so divine,*
> *Demands my soul, my life, my all.*[12]

We can trust our hearts to a God like this.

# CHAPTER 10

## welcoming change

Then the heart of Éowyn changed, or else
at last she understood it. And suddenly her
winter passed, and the sun shone on her.
—J. R. R. Tolkien, *The Return of the King*[1]

*January 8, 2021*

Today I accidentally called my daddy.

I haven't done this in more than four years. I guess it was inevitable since he's still in my "favorites" on my phone because . . . *nostalgia*. I have his last forty-one voice messages saved in my phone, too, ranging from 2014 to 2016 when he was still able to call me. I can't bring myself to listen to those, yet.

I thought I was calling my husband until it rang and rang, and I looked down at my phone and realized what I'd done. The endless ringing, as if to say, "He won't be answering you again," as if I needed that hint to know. Daddy used to love to call me. That is just one of the many things I miss.

But life moves on; this is now, and as I finish this book, we are in the throes of remodeling our fifty-year-old house. Dad was my hype man, so you can imagine how many times I've wanted to tell him what I'm designing or take him out and show him something I've worked hard on to get his approval. "Lisagirl, you've outdone yourself this time," I imagine him saying in his impassioned way. No one made me feel more like a smart and capable woman than my father did. That is one of the hardest things I've found about losing someone who was integral in your life: you have to replace the spot they filled for you with something else powerful. Don't misunderstand me to say you replace *them*. You never do that. You replenish the emptiness. Otherwise, you are just left with that gaping hole.

Change is attached to this loss of my dad. I've realized that one doesn't come without the other. What I've also realized is that when the change is unwelcome, it is particularly difficult. It may well be the hardest thing any of us face, which is why it is this book's final chapter. Everything we've talked about will require some type of change, or it will be the glorious byproduct. I want us to know up front that even if we are tired of the way we have been living and crave something else, we might still struggle to make the necessary adjustments to get there (aka imperfect journey). So don't get discouraged and quit. Stay in it and keep going. If we can get on the other side of change, we will love it.

It's just that darn getting there.

It's funny in a way because fighting change is what we often do, but almost always we are fighting what is best for us. Even if the initial hard thing (like a painful loss) isn't the good thing, in and of itself, healing from it will require we change something in our mind or heart, undoubtedly, which *will* be for our best. Change is where we make progress, where we get better. It is where we enjoy the benefits of breaking bad habits and finally living free. It's where we get that new us we've always wanted. It's where God is able to do that great work in us we have been anointed and appointed for all our lives.

It's where our hard days finally get to see their true worth.

## When It's Worth It

I delivered two things between July and September of the year 2000. One was hard and good. The other was just hard.

First, the just-hard thing: a kidney stone in month seven of my pregnancy of baby number two. Having never before experienced a stone, I self-diagnosed the dull, constant back pain as labor and breathlessly begged my mother to drive me to the hospital, sure I was moments away from giving birth. As luck would have it, my husband was out of town, my mother-in-law had just gone to the beach, and my father-in-law was left holding the card that forced him to take care of my then two-and-a-half-year-old, in the stage of life when wearing his *Blue's Clues* shirt was chief of the many things he was unwilling to budge about.

"This is bad," I managed to eke out between groans as I writhed from seat to seat in the back of the empty van, trying desperately to find relief. Had I known it was a stone and not my baby trying to come early, I would have recognized the futility of pain-management repositioning in this situation. If you've had one, you know.

After some Cruella De Vil driving—thank you, Mom—we arrived at the hospital, where I plopped into an awaiting wheelchair. Immediately wheeled into a room, I was checked for labor status and, to my surprise, discovered I wasn't in it. "I suspect a kidney infection or even possibly a stone," the doctor said, after getting me comfortable. "And here's a strainer for when you use the bathroom, to catch it." Then he added, "Just in case."

Convinced there was a mistake and no such stone existed, moments later I was proven wrong. I'll spare you the sordid details, but let's just say after some time I gave birth to an unattractive, round object I never liked well enough to name. For the sake of this story, we will call him "Rocky." (*Ba-dum-bum.*)

Still struggling to find the good in this.

Next came the hard and good thing, the delivery of my precious baby son about three months later. It was hard, the hardest of all my deliveries by a long mile. He was nine days late, overbaked, with plenty of time spent in there to rack up nearly nine pounds. My snuggly, loving boy was happily gestating and in no hurry to face things out here, while I, especially after the kidney-stone debacle, was in a big hurry to deliver something I actually liked.

After a failed epidural, a cranky doctor, and an intense labor that resulted in weeks of me traveling around with a Walmart plastic doughnut, Micah James Whittle was born, chubby and sweet. He was such a good baby from the beginning that I nearly forgot the whole hard, laborious thing. I didn't forget, though, because it was so hard. But the result was so good that the hard was well worth it.

When it's worth the sweat of the hard for the sweet of the good, that's the hard good. I suspect you're like me and not so much against the sweat unless it's for no good reason. If we are going to sweat, we don't want it to be for naught. "It's pain that feels pointless, pain without any purpose. That's the kind of pain that is so unbearable" is how pastor Rick Warren puts it.[2]

This is what I hope you have come to see through all we've talked about—there's

> *When it's worth the sweat of the hard for the sweet of the good, that's the hard good.*

an important *why* in holding this tension of the hard and the good. It isn't *just life*. God has a special and specific purpose in asking you to go down the challenging road. He wants to do His greatest work in you.

This will require you getting uncomfortable at times. It will require you showing up when you want to shut down. It will require that you finally come to a place of acceptance for the things you wish were something different. I could go on with the list—we've covered them in the chapters you've read.

What I hope I've shown you is that He will be with you all the way and, in fact, has led by example. The most challenging road has already been traveled down. If we allow Him, He will be in the center, helping it work together, even when our plans don't work out. Holding us together. Building us better, brick by brick. This is earth life, and He told us it would be so.

And what do I hope—perhaps you know—the most? That it will be *for you*. Anything hard you face, God wants to use to bring you personal joy and make you most usable for Him. This will be your greatest fulfillment, and, as my friend from chapter 6, Beth, said so truly, "the only way [we] can continue." Whether or not we have had a major life grief like hers, at some point we will all hit a wall we can't overcome without knowing our struggles serve a bigger purpose. Life fulfillment is only one thing: becoming the exact person God intends.

Though we want only the good, the Lord is wise to the full picture of our struggle. The risk of living in either the just-hard or the just-good is we would never learn the fullness of leaning on God.

In the tension we need Him the very most.

Undoubtedly there will be moments one or the other takes precedence in our lives. There will be times of goodness, and we will not want to hear about anything hard, as if realities awaken the sleeping giant of trouble. Then there will be other times life is so hard we won't allow ourselves to believe any of our hard has the possibility of a redeeming good. And yet, even if all we can hang on to is the promise of heaven when we need relief from our difficulties on earth, there the good lives. For the believer in Jesus, no amount of hard can ever strip away that good, solid, eternal promise. It is enough.

*The risk of living in either the just-hard or the just-good is we would never learn the fullness of leaning on God.*

Only His perspective makes our hard also good at the same time. In the latter days of my daddy's life, he would often say, "I am happy." This made no literal sense. The man couldn't walk. He couldn't comb his own hair. He could get out very few words. Yet the wild man of his youth had been tamed. His restless heart was settled. That's where his happiness came from.

This is what it looks like when Jesus does His greatest work in us. We change. We grow. We crave the way of Christ. His good begins to feel good to us.

True *spiritual transformation*.

### ℘ GOOD: ℀
**Welcoming in the new day will release you from wishing away the rest of your life . . . wanting back yesterday.**

*Everyone wants to be someone—someone who matters, someone who counts and leaves a mark on this world. But we don't become "someone" by chasing purpose.*

223

Maybe you've never thought of it this way. God has already decided you are a someone, and He already has a great purpose built in your life. So chasing what has already been predetermined will result in you constantly feeling empty and exhausted. It's an unnecessary scramble, a bit like trying to hurry and get your reservation in for a table at a restaurant, when your friend beat you to it, and your name is already on the list.

Your friend, Jesus, has already decided you have a great purpose here on earth. No need to scramble to try to find it. (See chapter 2 for a reminder of what that purpose is.)

Instead, focus on your usability, which, remember, is up to you. How usable you are will depend on how much you stick with Jesus through the uncomfortable process of being transformed by the hard-good things in your life. The things we talked about in the book are some of the main ones. Hard are the circumstances. Good is the result, when you don't run away from the discomfort of being shaped by the hard into maximum effectiveness. So you see, hard and good really are a holy pair.

Usability will bring you the best life. Being used by God results in the happiest human beings. No single other thing delivers more joy or satisfaction. It all boils down to allowing your struggles to drive you to your greatest usability for God. The way we get from struggles to usability is through change. And change arrives as we embrace the hard good.

*The way we get from struggles to usability is through change. And change arrives as we embrace the hard good.*

Maybe, then, change isn't so bad after all, right?

You don't have to let the hard good transform you. You can absolutely run away as King Saul did. But I hope you won't. I hope God has used all we've talked about in all these pages to show you why this is your best and most important life process.

I encourage you, as your first step in this transformational process, to stare down the legacy of your past and your very DNA. It is a crucial aspect of change that we can easily bypass. Don't start from where you are now. Start from where you started. (Not to stay stuck but to learn and move on.) I've documented much of my own journey with this in these pages.

Legacy and DNA are powerful. And confusing. Some of us run from the past we knew while others never knew our past and run around with the ache of not knowing it. We cling to it and we resist it, sometimes at the same time. I grip the pulpit like my father. Make his same facial expressions. Have the same fire that set his ministry ablaze. The same tendency to start things, get bored, and walk away. The same insatiable love for mayonnaise and bread, which always had us both carrying around extra weight. The great things and the not so great.

I love being like my father, and, at the same time, it terrifies me to death.

The question for all of us, with regard to change and the transformational process—especially if we struggle with a family legacy or DNA—is *where do I start and end?* There are two things you must realize quickly so you can move forward in health:

1. You are not merely your DNA or your family's legacy.
2. You will never be able to completely wash away that part of your story.

But story is not the same as legacy. This distinction became very important to me as I stared down my own family's legacy and gene pool.

My father died at seventy-five, having accomplished many things. He also left for heaven with unrealized talents and years of being sidelined by mistakes, as well as choices that took chunks of his influence and ministry. In my view (albeit limited), he never lived up to his full potential.

When my father moved us from church to church when I was young, in the name of family love and loyalty, we accepted that "God was calling us away." And maybe He truly was. But we also all *knew*—knew about the restlessness and running. I happily took my Miss Piggy poster and stuck it on the wall of every new room right away, creating my sense of home. Mom smiled as she happily cooked meals in every new kitchen as though we'd always lived there. My brother, Mark, happily read his encyclopedias and hunted for frogs in new yards as if he knew all the secret places they would hide. I loved my strange, wonderful childhood. It's all a lot of us have, I suppose.

But years later, when I'd grown up and had a life of my own, I could see it for what it was. Loving my past (I truly loved my childhood) didn't mean I also couldn't be honest about it. This was important for me, as it is for you, because it brings freedom. Telling the truth about the hard of our past does not dishonor the good that came with it.

I understand that sometimes our past does a real number on us. For many years I lived with the silent fear that, just like my father, I would never be able to settle, never be willing to stay put when serving Jesus became challenging. I figured at some point I would have to pick between my ability and my humility because one would surely take over. I never spoke this aloud, nor did I share my concern that, like my father, my influence might be cut short because of my own shortcomings.

> *Telling the truth about the hard of our past does not dishonor the good that came with it.*

One day I could fall just as fast and hard, and it would all be over in a puff of smoke.

Welcoming in the new day will release you from wishing away the rest of your life . . . wanting back yesterday.

These worries haunted me. For years they talked me out of going into ministry.

They made me afraid to write. And when I finally did, they tried to talk me into quitting.

They made me afraid to speak, which for years I ran away from.

They made me waste a lot of time wrestling with God over things I didn't need to wrestle over, things that were not about me but about the legacy I feared was my destiny. The DNA I feared would prevent me from staying true to the call of God.

Here I thought it was always living in the shadow of a perfect mother. But really it was my fear of becoming just like the father everyone said I was exactly like, who had it all and lost it, that scared me the most.

Can I tell you something I realized? It doesn't work like that. You don't become who you are merely by being born into it, because you have someone's blood inside your veins and a certain last name.

You are *you*, and you get to decide if your struggles will drive you to be used by God or drive you more into your own world. You get to decide if you want to change. You get to say if you will let the hard of your life be made good by God.

We cannot escape our past. But we can make peace with ourselves.

I hope for someone this comes as good news.

---

## A Precious Transformation

That baby I birthed in 2000 is now twenty. Recently Micah asked, "Mom, when I get engaged one day, will you let my fiancée ride in the front seat of the car when I'm driving, or will you expect to sit in the front?" Apparently this was a debate about moms versus fiancées on Twitter, and he wanted to know my hot take.

"Of course I'll ride in the back, honey," I told him, swallowing hard.

Welcome to my life of birthing to raising to letting go—living in the hard and holy tension. I'm doing this not only with my Micah but with my beloved firstborn, Graham, about to get married, and my youngest, Shae, the last one to go off to college, my darling best friend.

I'm learning that the more God changes us, the more we are able to pass on the gift of dying to self.

And the gift goes on. And the world sees God.

We give in generosity, and we get more back. We hand over, and we gain. Sometimes things do feel like death at the time, but it is that self-death that makes us better.

Another thing I've surely learned about change: if you do not embrace it, you will be overcome by the sadness of it. So much better to at least treat it like it is your idea. Or maybe I just like to boss things like that ☺.

I'm also learning that hard things can make us, not kill us.

It is all in the way we choose to usher them in.

God's gifts can be wrapped in change. That change can be hard. *They are still gifts.*

What if we began to view change as precious transformation? Instead of staring at what we've lost, we gaze at what we've *found*.

On the opposite end of King Saul, who ran away from God's uncomfortable yet transformational process, and, as a result, God was never able to do His greatest work in and through him, is King Josiah. According to 2 Kings, "Never before had there been a king like Josiah, who turned to the LORD with all his heart and soul and strength. . . . And there has never been a king like him since" (23:25 NLT).

I know who I want to be like. Usable in the most powerful way.

I don't want to become bitter because of the changes or the hard things in life. I want to become better. Even more, I want to be the one who turned to the Lord with all my heart and soul and strength in every single struggle.

You with me?

## You'll Be Okay

If you follow and trust Jesus and you are reading this sentence right now, I want you to know something. You are going to be okay. I give that qualifier, *if you follow and trust Jesus*, because it's the only way I can make such bold promises.

You are going to get out of this hard place someday and journey to a much better one. You are going to stop crying. You are going to never struggle again. You are going to experience only good and nothing else hard. This is the promise of heaven, and it is yours. So go through life believing this, my friend. You don't have to just hope it will all work out. *It will.*

In the meantime things will be very earthly and very human. So please expect those complications. I always amaze myself when I expect more from this life than what it can actually give me. I'm working on that.

I read your emails and messages, so I know your world is hard. Estrangements from children, deaths of loved ones, porn addictions, cancer, bankruptcy, eating disorders . . . the list goes on and on. We struggle to see past this moment, fight to reimagine what the rest of our lives could be—*past this*.

But God is in *this*, and the next this, and every this. Will we welcome His tender hand to change us in *this* process?

Please note: trusting Him to change us is not the same as understanding His methods. I well know.

I want to tell you one last thing: *God can change you.*

No, really. He can.

He can change your mind about things you've thought for years. Change your mouth about things you've said for so long. Change your heart about things you've privately held on to.

It's okay to let Him do that. You aren't losing anything by doing it except a part of yourself that hasn't served you well. Your self-protection hasn't protected you—you're still hurting. Your walls haven't kept the hard things out. Your routines of the past may carry the comfort of familiarity, but with that has come enormous wear and tear.

Your words in the past might have been pain talking. Your mind might have prompted you to take escape routes just to avoid the hard roads. Your heart might have been too stubborn to know the good that God knew but you didn't yet.

*I know.* For many years, in my effort to give myself an out in case I got bored or something in ministry got too hard, I would say to people as a qualifier before committing to any leadership role I was about to take, "I'm a builder, not a maintainer." I was proud to know myself so well that I was able to define my weakness as well as my strength. And it is true: with my visionary brain I do build better. But that wasn't why I said it. I needed the disclaimer in case I wanted out.

What I really was, was on the road to becoming just like my favorite person, my father. Running away, yet again . . . and again.

Change for me has been a constant process of staying in it with God and letting Him renovate and restore me. As I find myself knee-deep in the renovation project to our old house we just bought to fix up, I am struck by the parallels: tearing down to build back up . . . it looks worse before it looks beautiful . . . without a solid foundation, everything will crumble to the ground. Oh yes. I know something about all of these.

Without God's intervention, I would've quit on my marriage. I would've quit the ministry. I might've quit on a million different things.

Without His change, I would not have gotten better when my heart broke. I never would have shown up when I wanted to shut down.

Without His change, you won't be able to do hard things either. But with it we can become the people we were truly meant to be.

> So you *used to be* just a builder . . . but by God's grace He's now made you a maintainer too.
> So you *used to* have trust issues . . . but He alone has made you hopeful for your future.
> So you *used to* run away from hard things . . . but now you walk through them.

> Jesus has you. He is good.
> So, too, are you.

*August 31, 2020*

This is Mom and Dad's fifty-fifth wedding anniversary. *Would have been* if Daddy were still here. As irony would have it, I am at the ranch with Mom and Bonus Dad, John.

John takes Mom and me out for a ride in his camo Kawasaki early in the day before it gets to over one hundred degrees. *Why have I come to Texas in August?* I have asked myself at least five times since landing here on a plane some days ago.

We've been riding for a while when John spots something and

starts driving faster. "I want to show you something," he says, which is not an unfamiliar phrase for someone who grew up running through South Texas tall grass and knows the features of the land more intimately than most know their own pet dogs. I assume he wants to show me a plant and discuss its origin, or an animal on the land so he can tell me all about it. (Most recently, it was a horned toad.) The last time he had to show me something out here it was a longhorn's dead carcass, and I could already smell it for at least a mile before we got there. I silently pray this isn't another dead, smelly something.

A worn deer stand comes into view.

We pull closer, right up next to it, and John whirls the Kawasaki to a stop. I wait, knowing a story will soon unfold. Sweat drips from my forehead. John can tell a story or six, and I've grown to love them, but I have grown to love air-conditioning even more in this sweltering weather. He starts right in with his signature "Okay now," points up to the metal boxlike stilted stand, and continues, "Did I ever tell you the story about your dad and me hunting together when he used my gun to kill that big deer?"

John had, in fact, told me this one—probably a half-dozen times, but I loved it. As the story went, my father had gone out and bought a fancy new gun to take hunting with John, back when they were both young pastor friends. As they sat in a deer stand together, waiting on the perfect deer to come into sight, a large one appeared and Dad grabbed the closest gun to make the kill. It wasn't until it was all over that John noticed the gun in Dad's hands wasn't his own fancy new one, but John's old beat-up gun. John and my dad laughed for a long time about the irony of the situation. After all Dad's careful planning, the fancy gun hadn't even been necessary. John's did the trick just fine.

"You see those two seats right up there?" John's words interrupt my thoughts. I do see them, such as they are. They're pretty beat-up at this point, the fabric torn and tattered, weathered by the brutal Texas sun. "Those were the two chairs your dad and I were sitting in when that story happened. They weren't out here though. They were in an old hunting truck I used to have. I brought that stand out here."

It's funny what happens inside you when you connect with a piece of your soul's lost history. Immediately I feel tears beginning to well up. "You mean to tell me, John, that my dad sat in that chair?" I point to the one on my left.

"Yes, that's exactly where he sat. He sat right there."

And now, here we *all* sit, inside that sweaty Kawasaki—Mom,

John, and I—for what seems like an hour but is probably only a few minutes, nothing but the howling of Texas wind, sweat dripping, staring at two empty chairs, silent with our memories of a bigger-than-life man who is no longer here. For just a minute I think maybe if we stay here long enough, I can wish him into that chair.

Finally I find words and break the silence. "Can we scoot back a little so I can take a picture?"

John gives his signature enthusiastic "Sure!" We take off to reposition perfectly in front for the photo. "Let me open up the seats so you can really see them." John has a penchant for good aesthetics and accommodation, so he hops out of the Kawasaki without waiting for me to agree. He hikes over and reaches up, stretching on his toes to open the chairs. In my vivid imagination I can picture him and Dad as young hunters, laughing over a gun, sitting there together.

I want a photo of just the seats, but before I know it, the words tumble out. "Stand there and let me get your picture beside it." John is happy to oblige. He stands proudly, smiles, and poses for the shot.

My heart is both broken and full. Like so many times since Dad's death and the events that followed, I live in the tension of hard and good, carrying both joy and sorrow. I have won the lottery with my beloved bonus dad, John, and I have lost it all with my beloved daddy being gone.

Since my daddy went to heaven and my mother married John—a man I barely knew three years ago, whose past and present life and memories are inexplicably tied with mine—I have been living in this weird, wonderful world that I could not have survived if Jesus hadn't made it unbelievably possible.

John hops back into the vehicle, and we take off with a jerk. One thing is for sure, he drives like my daddy. And, of course, that is not where the commonalities stop. Jesus sure has a sense of humor to have made these two men that my mother and I both love so different and yet so very alike. I love them both for wearing boots and too much cologne, and for moving with swagger. I love them for their love of God's creation. When I'm with John at his ranch, and he's telling me about this bird or that plant, I feel my dad especially near. It makes no sense. And yet because I know and trust in the sovereignty of God, it makes all the sense in the world.

John can't hear well, so he yells over the hum of the Kawasaki as we drive along, "I know you love knowing your daddy sat in that seat." Obviously he's still thinking about it too.

And then I just say them, the words that are rising up from the deepest, tenderest place in my heart. "Yes, I love that. But I also love knowing you sat in that other seat. You're in the other seat of my heart now."

John smiles and chuckles in the way I've come to know and love. But he heard me. That I know.

I can't explain to you in perfect words how God makes hard things good.

What I can tell you is somehow He does.

# acknowledgments

Every time I think of you, I give thanks to my God.
—PHILIPPIANS 1:3 NLT

Scotty: Thank you for being trustworthy for twenty-five years. Thank you for never stopping the pursuit, never being unwilling to reconcile a fight, always being proud of me. Same team for life.

Graham, Micah, and Shae: I still feel taken when you walk into the room—can't believe I get to be your mom. Grown versions of you are the best versions. I even secretly love it when you make fun of all my quirks.

Caroline: I love it that we share an affinity for home décor and cafeterias. I especially love that you love my son and love our family since that first wild trip to the ranch. Crazy about you.

Mommy: Everyone loves you, but I get to call you mine. I know how truly kind you are . . . how truly selfless you are . . . how much you truly love Jesus. It's better than anyone on the outside knows. Daddy may have been my favorite person, but you are my anchor, compass, and strength—the person, besides Jesus, that I've needed the most my whole life. I love you so much.

Colleen: Almost nothing in my life has endured like our friendship. Without question, it is one of my life's greatest gifts.

Richard and Dianne: What a blessing to have in-laws who support me as you do. I love you.

Lainie: Thank you for juggling 256,048 things and always saying "I'm on it!" when I text you with one more. Thank you for sending me my Zoom password for every single meeting because you know me too well. And thank you for your support, prayers, and service to Jesus. I adore you, so please never leave.

Angie: Thank you for Lainie and also for being almost the same person as me and for long voxes.

The OG Intern Team: Sarah Farish, Tabitha Panariso, Jordan Wilkes, Macall Bennett, Sarah Zobel, Shannon Geurin, CiCi Kemp, Bridget Singleton, Kaitlin Rogers, Noelle Rhodes, Renee Gowler, and Maggie Yow, God chose you for the job, and you have done it with joy, conviction, passion, and dedication. We co-labored for a good work this year, and I'll never forget it.

Alli: Grateful to be your friend and partner in serving women to answer the call on their life. Thank you for memes and GIFs, Google docs, and basically being my Web MD.

Lisa Jackson: So much love and trust for you. You are one of the few people I'd let boss me on just about anything. Thank you for taking this journey with me and for having my back all the way.

Caleb and Unmutable: Not only are you ridiculously talented, but you are some of my favorite people to do life and ministry with—more than colleagues. Same brain. Thank you for being who you are and doing what you do. Your impact on this ministry is immeasurable.

Debbie: I love you, my friend. To think that God brought us from my random inquiry on a publishing website in 2006 to full circle with you as editor on this project before your retirement in 2021 is simply precious and divine. What a champion of the gospel you are. What a personal champion to me. Thank you. Go ride those horses and love life.

Lysa TerKeurst: Twenty years of friendship, my sister, and here we are. Thank you for this beautiful foreword. You were the one to write it. Thank you for always being gracious with what you know and have lived. We are all better for it.

W Publishing Team: To be led and supported by you, Damon Reiss, is such a privilege. Never known a finer publisher. Stephanie, Paula, Caren, Laura, Allison, Chris, Beth, Sara, I pinch myself to work with all of you. Thank you for enduring my long emails.

LW Write Club: You were there with this book in the trenches. Thank you for letting me show up unedited, unfiltered, and often sans makeup to share my heart about this book. I dedicate every word to you because you are my truest people, and we are doing the hard good together.

Jesus Christ, lover of my soul. Faithful, powerful, constant, good. I am more sure of you today than I have ever been. No matter what culture does, I will preach You until the end.

# notes

Chapter 1: Accepting Something You Wish Were
Something Different

1. Eugene H. Peterson, "Pain," *Holy Luck* (Grand Rapids, MI: Wm. B. Eerdmans Publishing Co., 2013), 18. Used by permission.

Chapter 2: Cheering for Someone When They Get What
You Want

1. Lana Del Rey (@LanaQuote), "When someone else's happiness is your happiness, that is love," Twitter, April 5, 2013, 8:20 p.m., https://twitter.com/lanaquote/status/320345301439361024?lang=en.

Chapter 3: Showing Up When You Want to Shut Down

1. Henry David Thoreau, *Walden* (1854; repr., London: Macmillan Collector's Library, 2016), 36.
2. Kirsten Nunez, "Fight, Flight, Freeze: What This Response Means," Healthline, February 21, 2020, https://www.healthline.com/health/mental-health/fight-flight-freeze.

Chapter 4: Doing What God Wants Even When It
        Disappoints Others

1. Lecrae Moore (@lecrae), "If you live for people's acceptance, you'll die from their rejection," Twitter, August 14, 2012, 8:37 a.m., https://twitter.com/lecrae/status/235369514517286912.

2. Dietrich Bonhoeffer, *Letters and Papers from Prison*, rev. ed., ed. Eberhard Bethge (Munich: Christian Kaiser Verlag, 1970; New York: Touchstone, 1997), 387. Citations refer to the Touchstone edition.

3. C. S. Lewis, *The Problem of Pain* (1940; repr., San Francisco: HarperSanFrancisco, 2001), 46.

Chapter 5: Finding Joy in the Waiting

1. Ernest Hemingway, *The Old Man and the Sea* (1952; repr., New York: Scribner, 1996), 83.

2. Quoted in Javhlan Amgalanbaatar, "The Suffering Olympics," *Harvard Crimson*, April 15, 2020, https://www.thecrimson.com /column/daring-to-be/article/2020/4/15 /amgalanbaatar-suffering-olympics/.

3. Hemingway, *The Old Man and the Sea*.

Chapter 6: Making Peace with Life When It's Brought Loss

1. Gerald Sittser, *A Grace Disguised* (Grand Rapids: Zondervan, 2009).

2. John Green (hankgames), "Lars Ulrich: The Miracle of Swindon Town #12," September 26, 2011, YouTube video, 13:25, https:// youtu.be/hg7v8FgxY0M.

3. C. S. Lewis, *Till We Have Faces* (1956: repr., San Francisco: HarperOne, 2017), 351.

Chapter 7: Facing Tough Conversations and Uncomfortable
        Truths

1. Charles H. Spurgeon, "The Lesson of the Almond Tree" (sermon), April 7, 1881, CCEL, https://www.ccel.org/ccel/spurgeon/sermons 46.xxiii.html.

2. Lisa Bevere, *Godmothers* (Grand Rapids: Revell, 2020), 219.

3. Ralph Waldo Emerson, *Emerson in His Journals*, ed. Joel Porte (Cambridge, MA: Belknap Press, 1982), 206.

## Chapter 8: Opening Your Heart Again When It's Been Hurt

1. Flannery O'Connor, *Mystery and Manners: Occasional Prose*, selected and edited by Sally and Robert Fitzgerald (New York: Farrar, Straus and Giroux, 1969), 78.

2. Augustine, *Confessions*, trans. Henry Chadwick (Oxford: Oxford University Press, 2009), 218.

## Chapter 9: Saying I'm Sorry First

1. Lewis B. Smedes, *The Art of Forgiving* (New York: Ballantine Books, 1997), 178.

2. Lisa Whittle, *5-Word Prayers* (Eugene, OR: Harvest House, 2017), 57.

3. Whittle, *5-Word Prayers*.

4. Beth Moore (@BethMooreLPM), "Never underestimate the power of an apology," Twitter, November 8, 2019, 7:17 a.m., https:// twitter.com/bethmoorelpm/status/1192793287939284992?lang=en.

5. Jessica Simpson, *Open Book* (New York: HarperCollins, 2020), 400.

6. Unknown source.

7. Kenneth S. Wuest, *Wuest's Word Studies from the Greek New Testament* (1973; repr., Grand Rapids: Eerdmans, 2002), 1:47–48.

8. Larry Richards, *Expository Dictionary of Bible Words* (Grand Rapids: Zondervan, 1985), quoted in "Forgive/Forgiven - Aphiemi," *Precept Austin* (blog), February 9, 2020, https://www .preceptaustin.org/forgive-aphiemi-greek-word-study.

9. Isaac Watts, "When I Survey the Wondrous Cross," 1828, https:// www.hymanary.org/text/when_I_survey_the_wondrous_cross _watts.

10. Watts, "When I Survey the Wondrous Cross."

11. Cahleen Shrier, "The Science of the Crucifixion," Azusa Pacific

University, March 1, 2002, https://www.apu.edu/articles/the
-science-of-the-crucifixion/.

12. Watts, "When I Survey the Wondrous Cross."

## Chapter 10: Welcoming Change

1. J. R. R. Tolkien, *The Return of the King* (1958; repr., New York: Ballantine Books, 2017), 262.
2. Rick Warren (Saddleback Church), "Change the Way You Think About Pain with Rick Warren," April 8, 2019, YouTube video, 3:44, https://youtu.be/Btc31ssmpss.

# about the author

LISA WHITTLE is the author of eight books and is a sought-after Bible teacher. A pastor's daughter and longtime ministry leader in issues relevant to the church, Lisa is the founder of Ministry Strong and the popular *Jesus over Everything* podcast, which debuted in the top twenty-five Christian podcasts. Her love runs deep to see people pursue Jesus for life, grow deep roots of faith, and walk strong in the midst of a world that so often seems to have gone crazy. Lisa has done master's work in marriage and family counseling, is the cofounder of Called Creatives, and has been featured on numerous media outlets through the years. She and her family live in North Carolina.

# New Video Study for Your Church or Small Group

If you've enjoyed this book, now you can go deeper with the companion video Bible study!

In this six-session study, Lisa Whittle helps you apply the principles in *The Hard Good* to your life. The study guide includes streaming video access, video teaching notes, group discussion questions, personal reflection questions, and a leader's guide.

Study Guide with
Streaming Video
9780310138648

DVD
9780310138662

Available now at your favorite bookstore,
or streaming video on StudyGateway.com.

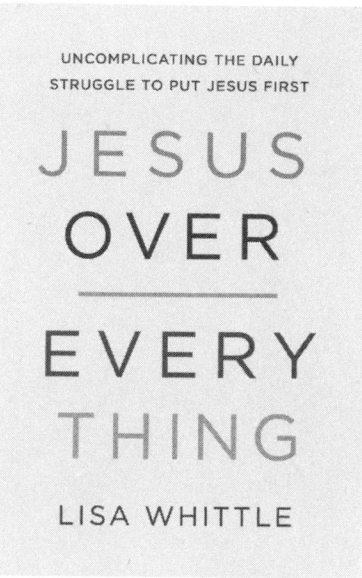

UNCOMPLICATING THE DAILY
STRUGGLE TO PUT JESUS FIRST

# JESUS
# OVER

---

# EVERY
# THING

## LISA WHITTLE

ISBN 978-0-7852-3198-1

In *Jesus over Everything*, Bible teacher, author, and speaker Lisa Whittle shares eight statements of choice to help us grow in our understanding of what it looks like to put Jesus first, whether our days hold power lunches, church meetings, sippy cups, or all three.

### DISCOVER THE JOY OF CHOOSING
- commitment over mood
- real over pretty
- steady over hype
- holiness over freedom
- service over spotlight and more

*Jesus over Everything* is a practical, compelling call to give God His rightful place in our everyday lives—so we can watch our everyday lives finally fall into place.